'This is the story of an examined life. Bill Freund tells us how Africa became the focus of interest of a smart Jewish kid from Chicago, about the obstacles the American academic establishment threw in his way, of his own evolving thinking about African politics, race, Marxism, and the role of the intellectual in society, and how he finally found a place for himself in university life and left politics in South Africa on the eve of apartheid's collapse. He has written an insightful and often moving account of the life of the mind in a time of political conflict.'
— Fred Cooper, Professor Emeritus at New York University and the author of *Africa since 1940: The Past of the Present*

'A beautifully told memoir that combines Bill Freund's love for travel with the curiosity of the historian. Freund's astutely-observed commentary on the societies in which he lived, his wry and yet empathetic accounts of people caught in the midst of the large political and economic movements of the twentieth century, and his unerring eye for the quirky and familiar make this an enthralling read.'
— Shireen Hassim, Canada 150 Research Chair in Gender and African Politics, Visiting Professor at WiSER, University of the Witwatersrand and the author of *Fatima Meer: Voices of Liberation*

'This is an extraordinarily honest and insightful memoir of the making of a worldly and theoretically savvy historian of South Africa. Bill Freund writes eloquently about his unconventional, and intriguing, personal and academic journey from Chicago to England, Nigeria and South Africa.'
— Steven Robins, Professor, Department of Sociology and Social Anthropology, Stellenbosch University and the author of *Letters of Stone: From Nazi Germany to South Africa*

T0385517

BILL FREUND

An Historian's Passage to Africa

An Autobiography

WITS UNIVERSITY PRESS

Published in South Africa by:
Wits University Press
1 Jan Smuts Avenue
Johannesburg 2001

www.witspress.co.za

First published 2021

http://dx.doi.org.10.18772/12021056727

978-1-77614-672-7 (Paperback)
978-1-77614-673-4 (Hardback)
978-1-77614-674-1 (Web PDF)
978-1-77614-675-8 (EPUB)

Project manager: Shaharazaad Louw
Copyeditor: Russell Martin
Proofreader: Tessa Botha
Indexer: Sanet le Roux
Cover design: Hybrid Creative
Typeset in 11.5 point Crimson

Contents

Foreword
Bill Freund and the Making of His Autobiography

In 1985 Bill Freund arrived in Durban as full professor and head of the Economic History Department at the University of Natal. At this point I was a lecturer in history at the neighbouring University of Durban-Westville, established exclusively for 'Indians' in terms of apartheid segregationist policy, and definitely the poor cousin of the much older University of Natal. I had not yet published an academic article or completed a PhD. Bill, by contrast, was already an accomplished academic, with global networks, over ten years of academic experience and two books to his name, one of which, *The Making of Contemporary Africa*, was described in the *Journal of African History* as 'a landmark in African historiography'.[1]

From soon after his arrival Bill became a close friend of mine. He also became my PhD supervisor and, in 1989, once I had joined the University of Natal, Durban, a colleague. It says a lot about Bill, Durban and the times that the personal and professional gulf between us did not prevent a strong and long friendship from developing. Bill was no snob and he welcomed all overtures of friendship. His arrival in Durban also coincided with an increase in levels of anti-apartheid activity, which created a community of like-minded people who knew one another and who welcomed Bill as a long-lost brother. Bill's views on apartheid, capitalism and injustice were well known, and he found himself among people who appreciated his views and were keen to involve him in academic and social life.

Increased repression, culminating in a national State of Emergency in 1986, cast a shadow over these times. The country was in the throes of what some at the time called a low-level civil war, particularly in KwaZulu-Natal. The heat was felt at the University of Natal where certain books could not be taken out of the Library (they were seen as a threat to national security) and forms of activism frequently attracted the attention of the security police. Yet, for all this, Bill began the happiest years of his life.

He became part of a group of mostly white, politically progressive men who played a game of touch rugby once a week.[2] He loved the game and the camaraderie, and seldom missed a session. Although he'd never played rugby before and his skills set was limited, the game made him feel manly. No longer on the sidelines and neglected, he was embraced as a team member. I think his happiness enhanced his writing and made him more confident.

The touch rugby game connected Bill with a number of high-profile activists, trade unionists, lawyers, doctors and academics. Bill's expertise was harnessed to the left-wing project of envisioning a post-apartheid society. He became part of Cosatu's Emerging Trends group, which discussed economic policy. His new life had a tempo and sociality that Bill was not used to, but he adapted quickly.

He built up the Economic History Department, giving it a profile and revisionist energy that it had never had before. He developed the postgraduate menu of the department and offered his supervision skills to those, like myself at the time, still embarking on a PhD.

I knew Bill as a supervisor, as touch rugby player, and as a man who loved ideas. In the years that followed, especially when I found myself as a lecturer at the University of Natal in 1989, I would have lunch every week with him at the staff club. Bill was interested in so many things that lunches were always lively. He was interested to talk about South African politics but, particularly after his mother died, he began to discuss his family and its history, about which you will learn a lot in this book. He was a good listener (although he preferred the role of raconteur) and he found my own history and family fascinating. There were some things that Bill wasn't much interested in, and this included my own interest in psychology and what Scott Peck called the road less travelled. And there were things that made him mad, including the increasing managerialism evident at the University of Natal (which Bill saw as ceding control of an academic institution to technocrats and managers). He also had strong and critical views about the quality of university students, as South Africa's transition advanced.

Bill's reputation was built on his writings about Africa, especially South Africa. It was from here that his primary academic affirmation came. And yet he sought recognition also from academics and scholars in the global North. He recognised the inequalities that divided North from South, identified with the position of writers in the global South, but never renounced his Northern roots. If anything, he sought to reconcile the possibly contradictory positions of being American and living, working and writing in Africa.

Bill's life came to an end prematurely. He was seventy-six years old. He had just had an operation to repair his wrist. He went home with a carer but two days later died in his own bed – an end that many would choose. Bill needed the operation because he had been involved in a very typical South African event, a mugging. Making his way by foot from his flat in Durban to the local shopping centre, Bill was confronted by a young man who demanded his wallet and cellphone. Bill, ordinarily timid, refused. He held onto his wallet but at great cost. He was flung to the ground, his shoulder was dislocated and his wrist badly broken. In an email to me on 29 August 2018, Bill wrote, 'You will be fascinated, Rob, to know that I felt a certain pride in resisting attack rather than just being a victim. I know it's foolish, but you know me well enough not to be surprised.' An initial operation failed to restore full mobility, and so he went into hospital for a further operation at a time when a national lockdown occasioned by Covid-19 was still in force.

While in hospital Bill's thoughts were still on his work. He was busy examining a dissertation, offering thoughts on the Industrial Commercial and Workers' Union (ICU) to Dave Johnson, planning for a chapter for inclusion in the *Oxford Handbook of the South African Economy*, co-edited by Imraan Valodia, working on a project of public housing with, among others, Alan Mabin, Kira Erwin and Monique Marks, and dreaming of the publication of his autobiography.

When Bill first shared the manuscript of his autobiography with me early in 2018, he had written it as three separate books. The first, which corresponds to the first three chapters of the present book, described his family roots. He had spent a number of years visiting eastern Europe, where he managed to trace his family history on his maternal and paternal sides to the seventeenth and eighteenth centuries. He discussed his approach with me:

> This first part of my memoir is a kind of pendant or prelude. It is partly an attempt to articulate in detail the values I learnt from family and family history but it is also an attempt to memorialise their world for which I have a strong attachment and some affection. It can be read separately from what follows and some of it consists of background that specialist historians will know as a matter of course. It also represents my personal attempt to address some of the problems associated with understanding the Holocaust which looms so large in the history of Europe in the 20th century.

In this first part one can detect Bill's search for belonging and place in the way that he describes the dispersal and decimation of his forebears. It also points to Bill's own story of how he found his way out of difficult situations and dead ends, and adapted to new circumstances.

The second part of the manuscript, which corresponds to chapters four to eight in the present book, Bill regarded as his autobiography proper. In it he tried to capture his political and intellectual experiences that shaped his adult years. What I find interesting is that Bill discovered a way here to forge a much closer relationship with his imagined readers than in his previous writing. Bill often inhabited a world where his ideas floated free of audience. This was why he was such an independent thinker – he didn't always imagine what the impact of his thoughts might be on other people. These could inspire, inflame or offend. Here, in his autobiography, he shows he was capable of an astonishing candour as he delved into his own life and sought to share it more widely.

Part three of the manuscript, which corresponds to chapters nine to eleven of the present book, deals with Bill's ascent to job security and academic recognition. When I, as a fellow historian and friend, read this part of the autobiography, I felt on more familiar ground. As the book shows, Bill had an enormous circle of acquaintances and friends. He moved easily in geographical, cultural and linguistic terms, and thus met and remained in contact with a very large number of scholars, many of whom were leading figures in African and southern African studies. Bill loved talking about ideas and, when people were not actually around to talk to, he would phone them or write letters (and later emails). It was in this way, and by accepting numerous invitations to travel and give seminars and lectures, that Bill built up an astounding global network.

Bill made an academic life and recorded it in this book. But, as his autobiography shows, he was also made by his circumstances and by his many acquaintances and friendships. This book is a tribute to Bill's life, tenacity, curiosity and his mastery of the historian's craft.

Robert Morrell
Cape Town
September 2020

Family Tree

Zehner-Kerdemann Branch

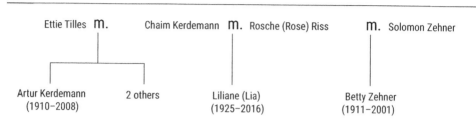

Ettie Tilles **m.** Chaim Kerdemann **m.** Rosche (Rose) Riss **m.** Solomon Zehner

Artur Kerdemann
(1910–2008)   2 others   Liliane (Lia)
(1925–2016)   Betty Zehner
(1911–2001)

Freund Branch

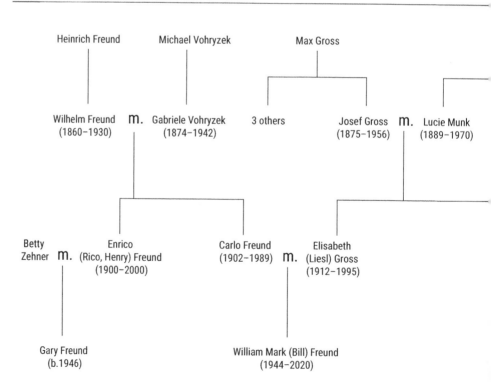

Heinrich Freund   Michael Vohryzek   Max Gross

Wilhelm Freund
(1860–1930) **m.** Gabriele Vohryzek
(1874–1942)   3 others   Josef Gross
(1875–1956) **m.** Lucie Munk
(1889–1970)

Betty
Zehner **m.** Enrico
(Rico, Henry) Freund
(1900–2000)   Carlo Freund
(1902–1989) **m.** Elisabeth
(Liesl) Gross
(1912–1995)

Gary Freund
(b.1946)   William Mark (Bill) Freund
(1944–2020)

Kemény Branch

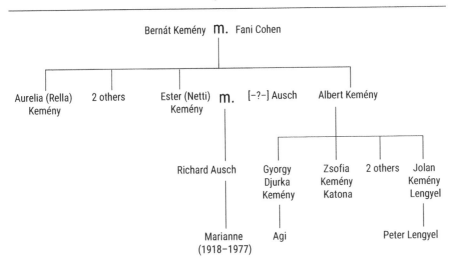

Bernát Kemény **m.** Fani Cohen

Aurelia (Rella) Kemény | 2 others | Ester (Netti) Kemény **m.** [-?-] Ausch | Albert Kemény

Richard Ausch | Gyorgy Djurka Kemény | Zsofia Kemény Katona | 2 others | Jolan Kemény Lengyel

Marianne (1918–1977) | Agi | Peter Lengyel

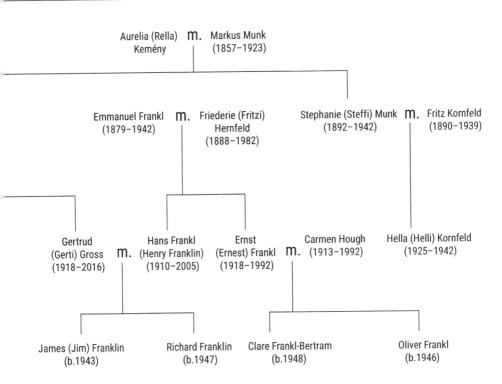

Aurelia (Rella) Kemény **m.** Markus Munk (1857–1923)

Emmanuel Frankl (1879–1942) **m.** Friederie (Fritzi) Hernfeld (1888–1982) | Stephanie (Steffi) Munk (1892–1942) **m.** Fritz Kornfeld (1890–1939)

Gertrud (Gerti) Gross (1918–2016) **m.** Hans Frankl (Henry Franklin) (1910–2005) | Ernst (Ernest) Frankl (1918–1992) **m.** Carmen Hough (1913–1992) | Hella (Helli) Kornfeld (1925–1942)

James (Jim) Franklin (b.1943) | Richard Franklin (b.1947) | Clare Frankl-Bertram (b.1948) | Oliver Frankl (b.1946)

A Brief Introduction

If they were born in the US to non-native parents, they are 'second-generation immigrants'. They have lived an authentically American experience, yet they carry the memes of foreign culture learned on their mother's knees, at their grandparents' table on feast days, from the strange old books and discrimination brought from the old country. They know the words of old songs. It may even be that second-generation immigrants feeling discriminated against, misunderstood and rejected by America, seek to immerse themselves in the culture and ideals of their parents' homeland, fabricating a hybrid identity for themselves based on an acquired reality they have never actually lived through, debased, idealised and simplified from the original.

– James Meek, *London Review of Books*, 5 January 2017[1]

For an American child of my time, I had a very unusual background. The particular combination of my parents and the situation in which I found myself was not only essential to what formed me but has driven me throughout my life. I was the son of refugee parents of considerable intelligence and life experience who came together, having found themselves lonely and stuck in a great provincial American city with little money and little sense of how to be a success in their new society, whose values were often very alien to them. They clung for a long time to the typical values of the society in which they had grown up.

It was probably fairly common for a child of central European refugees to want to access that route to success and aspire to a more prestigious and affluent life in America – and here I am not unusual at all. For an obvious example, the best-known William Freund you will find on the Internet was the chief economist of the New York Stock Exchange. He came from a German Jewish refugee family who built up a little business in New York after arrival from Nuremberg. He grew up in the same neighbourhood as Henry Kissinger, also from the Nuremberg area, and there are many like him. I was, however, a child with the kind of talent that led me to love books, politics, history, the past, words and languages, but with no aptitude for or connection with the business world. While I was hardly immune to some of the creature comforts of mass US post-war society, I was actually very much more taken up in the lost world that my parents valued and talked about. Perhaps the American bit that I did assimilate was my great dislike of authority over me personally. I didn't like the idea that I was a *tabula rasa*, coming from nowhere into a world of boundless opportunity. That is why I have written the first chapters of this book. It was important to me even as a child that I – my family – had a past before America. I had, moreover, a left view of society from the start, one I was brought up with and that I extended as I grew up. It clashed not only with dominant US values but also with my own contradictory desire for a more commodious and affluent life than my daily existence as a child allowed.

This led me to an idealised picture of what it would be like to be an academic, the route I chose early on. I not only chose it but was terrified of what would happen if this desire got me nowhere, with no sense of any alternative. It suffused me so fully that I pushed other feelings, other emotions, to the side all my life. My positive view of people very much required some sense of them acknowledging me positively in this regard. I can't say now that I care much that I never had a family of my own or even significant romantic relationships, because I never really had significant romantic feelings beyond the very superficial when I was young. By contrast, a feeling of inferiority and lack of success in terms of conventional masculinity, while far less prominent now than in my youth, never left me.

It does mean that, while I take much pleasure from travel, from many kinds of music, from art, literature, good food and drink, these are all accoutrements that fill in the spaces in my life and make it amusing and well balanced. The stuff connected with my intellectual life, especially what I write, is, by contrast, the essence that occupies most of my days and brings me satisfaction and a sense of accomplishment. I probably have a very exaggerated sense of my own intellectual originality and talent and the importance of my own work. However, what follows in these pages has been written in the hope that this side of me may attract some other people. In this book I attempt to explain the cultural and political foundations of my beliefs that infuse what I teach and write. In addition, I try to provide observations of the sharply distinct environments in which I have lived and worked.

All this goes together with a personality that is, as one South African woman friend once had the temerity and honesty to say, more egoistic, more deeply self-centred and selfish than most. I think that there is a distinction between egoistical and egotistic. I can be a nice guy in interacting with people I like, of whom there are quite a few, and I have friends of very long standing. I have no doubt, too, that in my way I have helped many people. But I also cannot imagine living for the love of another human being; that is what I mean by egoism. So this distinction only helps to provide a definition of me, a man who is deeply an egoist but not particularly egotistical. It is also what I see when I take an honest look at the mirror, in the classic tradition of Rousseau's *Confessions*.

It may seem appropriate to lard what follows with expressions of gratitude to friends at many stages, people whom I have enjoyed knowing or who were practically helpful to me at important moments. Where this importance had a bearing on my development, I have hopefully made some appropriate mention, but this is not so much to express appreciation of people that I like or have liked. To do that would make this document very tedious to readers, so my apologies where they are so often due. It is in the interest of making a book that is accessible to a larger number who, I assume, will be interested in me because of my ideas rather than one that is mainly an affectionate tribute to old friends.

I sometimes think of myself as Superman, admittedly without super powers. Almost all the time, I stay Clark Kent with no access to the phone booth to change into effective costume. But here was an iconic hero who did not fit in and whose parents had got him out of a distant galaxy that connected with little or nothing around him. The planet Krypton, which was about to be destroyed, was created in the comic books very fittingly in the year 1939. That pre-war Europe was my Krypton.

1 | The Austrian Past

The story of this Chicago-born American who would later settle in Africa and whose life's work sought to understand that continent starts in central Europe, for that is where my family came from. Theirs is mostly the story of Austrians, of Jewish people who lived in Austria both after 1918 and before then, when Austria was a vast continental empire of fifty million people and, as such, one of the Great Powers of Europe. My aunt Gerti, who died in 2016 close to the age of 98, must have been one of the last living individuals born a subject of Kaiser Karl and the empire, which collapsed when she was a few weeks old. Her husband, my uncle Henry, always remembered having once as a child seen Karl on horseback.

Taken as a whole, this was not a territory that, like Britain or Germany, had any chance of becoming a nation-state with a clear, generally accepted national identity. It was an empire like Russia or Turkey and what held it together was the ancient Habsburg dynasty, an estate-owning aristocracy from many different provinces, and a considerable and relatively efficient bureaucracy typical of the absolute monarchies of early modern Europe. The other element was the Catholic Church, the Habsburgs having identified themselves totally with the Counter-Reformation.

At the centre of the empire lay Vienna, in early modern times the biggest German-speaking city in Europe with a large and varied population of artisans, tradesmen and serving people who worked for the Habsburg ruling class. That class held estates all over the empire but desired palaces of their own in the walled city. Vienna was a city, like Paris, with a distinct flavour and a distinct urban culture where Baroque splendour largely effaced what remained of the Middle Ages.

In the early modern period, the Habsburgs had three glorious victories that complemented their famous policy of expeditious dynastic marriages, their lucky string of long reigns and their endless wars to defend the territorial gains that were consequently made. As a result of the Thirty Years War they acquired, among other things, the largely Czech-speaking provinces of Bohemia and Moravia. With their victory over the Turks in the late seventeenth century, they took control of all of Hungary. And at the end of the eighteenth century, by participating in the partition of the kingdom of Poland, they gained Galicia, a region that we could describe as deeply east European.

In all three regions there were sizeable Jewish minorities, and in all three instances of Habsburg expansion I have described, Jews fared quite differently. In the lands of Bohemia and Moravia, the capital of Prague had the largest Jewish community in the northern half of Europe, perhaps at times exceeding ten thousand people, with Frankfurt its only rival. After the partition of Poland, Austria acquired the region of Europe with the densest Jewish population of all. Here lived, even in 1918, some two-thirds of all Austrian Jews, a people culturally very distinct from their neighbours and very inward-looking indeed. Yet even here, especially in the twentieth century, there was a notable shift out of the ghetto culture.

In one important way, Jews were unlike any of the other 'nationalities' of the empire – the Czechs, Poles, Germans, Hungarians, Croatians, Romanians, Ukrainians and Italians. They were uninterested in claiming rights as Jews beyond the very local and, increasingly, the universal. To the extent that they had a wider allegiance, the empire was good enough. In the nineteenth century they justifiably acquired the reputation of being reliably *Kaisertreu*, loyal to the emperor and empire.

During the long nineteenth century stretching from the French Revolutionary wars to World War I, the influence of the Enlightenment led to a growing acceptance in ruling circles that Jews in the empire, as increasingly everywhere in western Europe, should be treated as citizens like anyone else; this became governing statecraft. Jewish historians seem to take this as an imposition, but it was far from unwelcome. In 1840 a major turning point occurred when the limitations on Jewish residence were entirely abolished; within a generation Jews were flocking to the cities. Finally, with the constitutional creation of the Dual Monarchy of

Austria–Hungary in 1867, the *Ausgleich* (Compromise), Jews received full civil rights.

Here began the *Gründerjahre*, the foundational years, the Austrian equivalent of the liberal French Empire in the late phase of Napoleon III or, even better, the whole Belle Époque that followed. In the late nineteenth century, the empire expedited the modernisation of the economy to an important extent. Cities grew fast; major industries were established. Vienna, even if overtaken by Berlin in size, became a *Grossstadt*, a metropolis.

The history of my family, who could be found all over the Austro-Hungarian empire, can be framed by two overriding and connecting themes. The first was the movement from village to town to city. The second was the success of thousands of Jewish-owned firms in becoming sources of wealth and economic dynamism. At the same time, the growth was, as always, uneven.

My mother's father, Josef Gross, and especially her maternal grandparents, the Munks, were archetypal success stories of the long reign of Emperor Franz Josef (1848–1916). The Munks came from the Moravian town of Boskovice, which is today a living museum. Despite some attempts at factory manufacture, Boskovice did not take off and many of its Jews left over the years, including my mother's beloved *Grosspapa*, Max (Markus), who seems from surviving correspondence to have been a very well-spoken and charming man. Max operated a business that sold leather and embroidered goods, specialities of Vienna, to wealthy visitors. He settled in Vienna as did so many Jewish merchants from Bohemia and Moravia, but in the summer he repaired to Marienbad, the famous spa town near the Bavarian border.[1] This was once a famous centre which gathered together the good and the great, who could meet there informally. One customer who often met his lady friends during his six seasons in Marienbad was the playboy Prince of Wales, the future Edward VII.

Max Munk was entitled to call himself *Hofleverancier*, purveyor to the court of England, as a successful merchant selling to royalty. He himself went to London on business in 1906 and stayed at the Savoy. Another customer was one of the very wealthy Indian princes who imitated the lives of idle and rich European aristocrats, the maharajah of Patiala. This was almost certainly Bhuphinder Singh (1891–1938), once famous for his

Figure 1.1: Premises of Markus Munk, Junior on the Stephansplatz (on the ground floor below Jacob Rothberger), with a Corpus Christi procession including the emperor, Franz Josef, under way

extravagance and his sporting prowess, sponsoring polo and cricket teams. He was supposed to be the first Indian to own an aeroplane, designed by the Wright Brothers, and to have fathered eighty-eight children by his many wives and concubines. He was considered by the British establishment to be the leader of India's Sikh community. However, my grandmother long remembered him as the maharajah who didn't pay his bills.[2]

In Vienna, the business was called Markus Munk, Junior, and was located on the Stephansplatz right opposite Vienna's cathedral, on the ground floor below the well-known department store of Jacob Rothberger.[3] My grandmother Lucie and her sister Stefanie, born in 1889 and 1892 respectively, often helped in the shop. These girls were quintessentially Viennese. Lucie went to a finishing school and was an accomplished pianist.

Max fell in love with and married a woman from a somewhat different sort of business background: Rella or Aurelia Kemény. Rella came from a big family in Somogy County, south-western Hungary. Her father was a successful merchant and grain miller in a district dominated by the

Figure 1.2: My grandmother Lucie and her best friend, Ella Erdös, 1910

Esterhazys. Her mother was unused to writing in Latin script; instead she normally communicated with her daughter in Hungarian but using Hebrew script – she still had a foot in the old school. Papa was an impressive patriarch and he decided on the marriage of his several daughters, with the exception of Rella, perhaps the youngest. When Rella passed the age of twenty, she came to visit her sister and her husband in Vienna. It was at their flat that Max and Aurelia met and, after their marriage, they remained in Vienna.

In 1910 their daughter Lucie would marry Josef Gross; these were my maternal grandparents. Josef had been born in 1875 in the capital of Galicia, Lemberg (Lwów, Lviv), where his father was on assignment for the state railways, although the family seems to have been domiciled already in Vienna. He went to school in Vienna and was a classmate and friend of the famous violinist Fritz Kreisler. Josef would wander further afield.

His successful import-export business would take him twice to the golden land: America. On the first trip he visited New York; the second time, in 1913, he went to Chicago.

By way of contrast to the members of the Munk and Gross families who benefited from the great social and economic changes in the empire, one could mention my paternal great-grandfather, Heinrich Freund. With a base in the tiny settlement of Drěvikov, a Bohemian village where Jews formed the majority of the population, he travelled through the German-speaking lands on horse and wagon, trading with peasant customers, buying and selling women's hair and women's clothing for instance. He struggled so that the younger son, my namesake and grandfather Wilhelm Freund, could attend grammar school in Hradec Kralové (Königgrätz), site of the decisive battle of the Seven Weeks War of 1866 in which Prussia defeated Austria. One of the boy's memories was being carried around by a Prussian soldier on horseback after the Prussian victory.

Wilhelm was born in another village, Načešic, and his future wife, Gabriele Vohryzek, in Dubany near Pardubice, not very far away. Victor Vohryzek, a native of Pardubice, was the activist who promoted Jewish identification with Czechs, Czech nationalism and the rising star of the liberal politician Tomáš Masaryk in the late nineteenth century. As a teenager, Gabriele Vohryzek was sent to a respectable Catholic finishing school in Prague.

Wilhelm Freund succeeded in making a remarkable move in his thirties. He obtained an appointment as a bookkeeper to a big industrial enterprise in northern Italy near Florence. His passport for use there is dated to 1898 though conceivably his work began somewhat earlier. It was in 1899 that he got to know Gabriele Vohryzek in Prague and he brought her to Prato, his new home, as his bride. Their honeymoon, reflecting the good times, unfolded on the French Riviera. In Prato their two sons, Enrico and Carlo, my uncle and father respectively, were born in 1900 and 1902.

The many tokens I have of their life in Prato, around the corner from the Renaissance cathedral, with its wonderful art by Donatello and Fra Filippo Lippi, are signs of sociability and pleasant opportunities of leisure.

Wilhelm was employed at the first modern textile factory in Italy, *il Fabbricone*. The factory, which was established by two Jewish Austrian entrepreneurs, Hermann Kössler and Julius Mayer, in 1887, ensured that

Figure 1.3: Michael Vohryzek, my grandmother Gabriele's father

Prato would become one of the largest industrial districts in Italy in the textile apparel sector.

Il Fabbricone, as it came to be known by everyone in the town, was a large factory with twenty-seven hundred workers at peak that made cloth and clothing. Originally it was intended to assist the new Triple Alliance of Austria–Hungary, Italy and Germany with the manufacture of uniforms. The workforce was largely Italian, but enough German and Austrian workers were resident to justify the existence of a German club in Prato that catered for technical personnel in particular.

The factory is an interesting site in Italian history apart from its economic importance to Prato and the textile industry. One humble worker, Gaetano Bresci, probably a contemporary of Wilhelm Freund, was an anarchist who emigrated to New Jersey. Inspired by the assassin of US

Figure 1.4: Wilhelm Freund, my grandfather, in Prato

President William McKinley, Leon Czolgosz, Bresci returned to Italy and proceeded to kill the unpopular Italian king Umberto I. Imprisoned, he died in murky circumstances the following year. However, the Italian left honoured him as a hero and a street in Prato (more recently a Communist stronghold) is named after him. *Il Fabbricone* experienced big strikes and employed many committed anarchists. This is the world of Bertolucci's great film *1900.*

In 1915 Italy was effectively bribed by Britain and France to break its historic tie with Germany and Austria (the government had already opted for neutrality) and enter World War I on the Allied side. As a result, *il Fabbricone* was administered by a syndicate and then sold to an Italian firm. One can only speculate what would have happened to the Freunds if they had remained in Prato.

But in 1905, sadly and reluctantly, they left Italy, as Wilhelm found himself suddenly paralysed from his legs down, unable to walk, perhaps caused by reaction to an infection. They stayed for a while in a little market town in Bohemia. Then in 1906 they put their savings into a little house in a place close to Vienna called Mödling, an ancient town, picturesque and near the vineyards of the Vienna Woods. They hoped the local sanatorium might offer him relief. There my father and his brother grew up; they were both very attached to the town. It is worth mentioning that they had no larger family roots in Mödling; all their kin were in Bohemia, some in Prague. This was in contrast to my mother's family, some of whom had settled in Vienna.

This era was remembered later with great fondness by many. In *The World of Yesterday*, the writer Stefan Zweig, himself the scion of a wealthy Viennese family originating from Moravian Jews, called it 'the Golden Age of Security'. One finds, above all, the sense that the state, the system, encouraged the growing prosperity and departure from the ghetto of these typical families. The political balance of the Dual Monarchy made them content to be living in an empire of so many nationalities. Jewishness was acceptable to the state, and it has been argued that discrimination there was less than that in contemporary Germany.[4] With some family members, one can see the beginnings of conversion to Christianity, but often this was at first simply a way of being able to avoid writing 'Jewish' on forms. There was little commitment to the Jewish religion or to any demonstrable Jewish ways for thousands of such families, but what is noticeable was a strong tendency to live within their own social milieu and, indeed, to marry in a way that helped cement business linkages. They loved Vienna and the big cities of the empire, but this meant for them respect for the state and for high culture and some aspects of less highbrow activities – the waltz, typical Viennese food and the like. All the same, they remained a distinct element vis-à-vis the old urban popular culture of the city (few liked to speak dialect – a populist touch of even the old emperor – as opposed to correct German) and they were not attracted to the Catholic Church. Moreover, as popular educational levels rose, there emerged a lower middle class characterised by the enthusiastic adoption of German – and, elsewhere, other – nationalisms; but this too was absent among Jews because such nationalisms, generally and more and more vociferously, did not embrace these new adherents. Instead, they refused to regard Jews as true Germans, Hungarians or whatever, and saw them as rivals blocking their advancement. This was widely accepted in the very successful Christian Social Party of the turn of the century.

In the summer of 1906, my great-grandmother Rella Munk sent a letter to her husband Max from the resort of Balatonföldvár on Lake Balaton in Hungary. 'We are not at all suffering from any anti-Semitism', she wrote, 'so long as one behaves in a peaceful and inconspicuous manner.' For once reference is made to the unpleasant reality that, despite the official rights Jews enjoyed legally, they were very unpopular with most of the Christian population; and at times from the last decades of the nineteenth century, incidents and public interventions brought this out. As Rella suggests, however, respectable folk with sufficient resources were invariably treated with a politeness and courtesy that did not necessarily express genuine feelings. This would continue and intensify. It was the imperial balance that held things in tension. Rella also gently chides Max for writing insufficiently, only once a week, which seemed just not enough compared with the ladies whose husbands would join them for a weekend of leisure from Budapest. Family feeling normally suffused social interaction. In virtually all correspondence, relatives had to be referred to as 'liebe', or dear, throughout and often the abbreviation l. was the normal polite substitute. Of course, behind this lay other realities sometimes, but these were too masked for me to decipher for the pre-war times.[5]

World War I began with the crisis engendered by the assassination of the heir to the Austrian throne. Lasting well over four years, the war ended in the destruction of the Austro-Hungarian empire, which collapsed into a number of would-be nation-states with varying records of success. At the end of the war, Vienna suffered from the ravages of the great flu epidemic and from serious shortages in a season of terrible privation.

My father and even his slightly older brother were just a bit too young to serve as soldiers. On the other hand, my mother's father, Josef Gross, then thirty-nine, came back from America, having failed to persuade my grandmother to accompany him as an immigrant there, and joined the Austrian army. From the postcards he sent to his little girl, my mother, it is possible to trace his movements up to a point. He seems to have spent the years 1915–1917 in Istanbul. He was *Oberleutnant* (lieutenant) responsible for organising the feeding of the Austrian troops fighting alongside the Turks – certainly at Gallipoli if he was there already in 1915. In February 1918, he was stationed in Krakow at a transit supply station feeding the combat troops much further to the east. My grandmother said that he had been too lenient with the British prisoners and perhaps this was the reason for the consequent move. From Krakow he was able to get leave to go home to Vienna, where my grandmother must have conceived her younger daughter, my aunt Gerti, in February 1918. Gerti was born a few weeks before the war ended. Feeding her and providing her with milk was a difficult task, and to this end Josef had to comb the outskirts of Vienna. This was a small sign, perhaps, of the difficulties that were to come.

2 | The Aftermath of War: A Perilous Modernity

The war was the end of the good times, the secure times. What remained of Austria was the rump republic with today's frontiers. Adjusting the economy to this new reality was a long, slow, harsh process. A frail, credit-dependent recovery lasted only until the Great Depression set in, bringing more hard times. The aristocrats left Vienna for the new countries where they held land in the former provinces. Vienna began a descent into provincialism. Its population, one-third of the total in the new country, started to decline and continued to fall for almost a century, until very recently. A more modern society struggled to emerge in a context where there were more losers than winners.

All the same, the Jewish middle class was better equipped, through its practicality and its educational qualifications, to weather the storm economically. *Grosspapa* Munk, more or less retired, would live until 1923 when he died, to the great sorrow of my eleven-year-old mother. She and her mother Lucie had spent the war years in his charge, while Josef Gross was away.

On his return from the army, Josef, having given up his own venture, became a partner in Markus Munk, Junior. After some time, the business in Marienbad was sold to a relative who was now a Czechoslovak and a new summer trade locale was taken up in the mountain spa of Bad Gastein in the south of the Salzkammergut. Over the years, this business did very well. The premises on the Stephansplatz were desired by a neighbouring café and the lucrative sale meant that the firm could move into the premier shopping street of Vienna, the Kärntnerstrasse, which runs between the Stephansplatz and the Opera.

Figure 2.1: Liesl Gross, my mother, aged nine, with her parents and grandfather on an outing to Baden bei Wien, 1921

My Gross grandparents rented a large apartment in Hietzing only five minutes' walk from the entrance to the grounds of the magnificent old summer palace of Schönbrunn. This was a desirable neighbourhood which was considered quiet and green. They employed a servant and, after the season in Gastein had ended, they took holidays in France, Germany and Italy during the 1920s. There was always a sort of governess with whom to leave the girls; the best-loved was Lizzi. Lizzi's mother was an impecunious aristocrat who would come to the flat and play mournful renditions of 'Glow, Little Glow-Worm' on the piano. As a gift, she gave my mother the collected letters of the Mendelssohn family. This story in two volumes of a much-revered Jewish patriarch and philosopher whose descendants all became Protestants, including his grandson, the great composer Felix Mendelssohn, reflected her perspective: they were fine people who had shed the undesirable Jewish qualities. This set is still in my possession.

My grandmother in time arranged another situation for Lizzi with the Herder family, who owned a prominent Viennese bookshop (which still exists on the Wollzeile). A proxy marriage was afterwards arranged with the younger son of the family in the Stephansdom (St Stephen's Cathedral), which the Grosses attended. Then Lizzi went off to live on a farm in South Africa, where he had settled, the one family connection with the country where I have come to live. On the Internet I was able to find a very charming photograph of Lizzi, who won a Mrs South Africa beauty contest in 1930.

My mother's scattered memories were of security and comfort. At midday, Papa took the streetcar back home for the main meal of the day prepared by the maid or, on her day off, by my grandmother, who was an excellent cook. In the afternoon, he returned to work and then went to his *Stammtisch*, or favoured café table, where he would discuss affairs and life

Figure 2.2: Lizzi Herder, my mother's governess, at her wedding in St Stephen's Cathedral before going to join her husband in South Africa

with his friends. Then, when they were young, he went home in time to kiss his daughters goodnight. My grandfather looked down on Jews who converted to Christianity in order to better themselves; he would have seen them as lacking self-respect. Once a year he repaired, just by himself, to the original Viennese synagogue in the Seitenstettengasse for New Year's services. However, his piety did not stretch so far as to keeping kosher. He famously provided the household on at least one memorable occasion with an exotic lobster, forbidden in Jewish dietary laws. He did like food and had the central European fondness for walks in the forests during the autumn to pick mushrooms. He loved America, which he had visited twice on business before the war, albeit failing to persuade Lucie to emigrate at the time.

The Depression came with a bang, marked by the collapse in 1931 of the Creditanstalt Bank, once the key vehicle of the Viennese Rothschilds. However, the business of Markus Munk, Junior survived. The premises on the Kärntnerstrasse were sold, and a smaller rented shop was taken around the corner on the Neuer Markt. By the mid-1930s some prosperity returned. The mixed fortunes of the Gross family, like those of many other parts of my extended family in a region of Europe in distress, give shape to the famous cliché of a world where everything was always in crisis but nothing really changed all that much.

Culturally, the affluent Jewish families of Vienna inherited the mantle of artistic patrons and were the heart of the avant-garde. More than ninety per cent of the two hundred thousand Austrians of Jewish origin, very diverse in background and tastes, lived in Vienna, where they formed over a tenth of the population, far more than in Berlin or Prague (though not Budapest). The strongest political force in the country was the Christian Social Party, which defined Austria as Catholic and had its greatest strength in the villages and towns in the provinces. While not all its luminaries were anti-Semitic, the thrust of the party was suspicion of Jewish claims of Austrianness; discomfort with the cultural supremacy of Jews such as Zweig, Schönberg and Freud, who were seen by foreigners as representative Austrians; and resentment at the apparent numerical dominance of Jewish businesses in many fields, notably banking and the media, and of Jewish professionals. The party pursued a usually unspoken intention to cut this questionable minority down to size.

There was also a challenge from secular German nationalist forces, which drifted towards affiliation with the German National Socialists.

The strength of this grouping was to some extent negated by poor organisation. An attempted coup which involved the assassination of Chancellor Dollfuss in 1934 failed but led to the suspension of the democratic constitution. The Socialists resisted – feebly – their loss of control in Vienna in the so-called *Bürgerkrieg*, civil war, later that year. Repression thereafter led to some Jews going into exile, but it could hardly be compared to the harsh treatment of the opposition in Nazi Germany or even Fascist Italy. The relatively limited character of repression was matched by the fact that Jewish-owned businesses could carry on as usual and Jewish youths continued to attend the university in Vienna. Many Jewish people, albeit nervous, lived in the afterglow of the old stable regime, whose laws continued to protect their civil state.

My father had been born in Prato in 1902, and he grew up with the most positive idea about Italy (or at least northern Italy). However, as we have seen, at the age of three he and his family left Prato and settled in the small and picturesque town of Mödling, to which he was also very attached all his life. Nearby is the Anninger mountain, a favourite Viennese walking destination. As is much truer today, it was an easy commuting distance from the capital. There was a small Jewish community, founded in the mid-nineteenth century. Just before World War I, a synagogue was dedicated in the presence of the old emperor and here my father would have been bar mitzvahed.

The Freunds had a small house bought with their savings, but they were at first very poor. Most Jewish families lived above or behind shops off the town centre, but the Freunds did not manage a business. My grandmother took in washing and my grandfather offered lessons to schoolboys. The situation only improved when the two boys grew up and started working. My father went to the *Volks-und Knaben Bürgerschule* (People's and Boys' School) and then was apprenticed as a clerk in the slightly larger town of Sankt Pölten under the aegis of the *Landesgymnasium* (provincial secondary school) until 1919. In this patriotic period, he was definitely a Karl.

Karl was a very handsome youth and the biggest boy in the class. In later years, he was often mistaken on the street for the right-wing aristocrat and politician Ernst Rüdiger von Starhemberg. He was, however, quite clumsy and not very interested in sport apart from enjoying watching boxing matches. Of course, he skied and skated and walked in the mountains. Just a few doors down the road, a well-known swimming bath was opened for the public in 1926 and the street was renamed Badstrasse in its honour. Apart from the pool with its three-metre diving board, it boasted a post-box, a newspaper kiosk, a gym, a bridge table and a special section for nude sunbathing.[1] This was clearly a hang-out and it attracted a crowd from far and wide.

As a young man, Karl was very popular. While he knew a few of his relatives from visits, none of them lived anywhere close by or, indeed, in Austria as it was now constituted. His brother Rico loomed very large in his life, barely two years his senior.

As he matured, Karl became Carlino especially for the girls. From 1922 he had work with the established Viennese furrier Teutsch. The late 1920s represented a very pleasant period of his life. Remaining papers and photographs indicate a visit to Capri and Naples in the summer of 1925, a trip to Czechoslovakia in the footsteps of his mother and brother, and a short stay in Budapest at the start of 1930. There were also various skiing and hiking trips. However, in late 1931 his old boss, Johann Teutsch, died and the old-established furriers' firm was wound up shortly afterwards at the height of the Depression. I don't know if he found work again quickly or when, but I think this marked the start of a period of hard times.

Figure 2.3: My father, Carlo Freund (top right), at the swimming baths next door to his home in Mödling, 1927

Wilhelm Freund, sent in 1928 to the Lainz sanatorium – established by the anti-Semitic social reformer, Karl Lueger, at the start of the century – had died in 1930. After this, my ageing grandmother lived with her two unmarried adult sons. Things seem to have improved in the mid-to-late 1930s. Rico, the elder son, met Betty Zehner at the well-known ski resort of Semmering, on the big railway line south of Vienna, and they formed a patient attachment that would lead to marriage eventually in America. As for my father, the main romance that emerges from surviving papers is with a dancer, Gerda Bauer. Carlo and Gerda were together on holidays several times in 1930–1931, but I have no idea what happened to this once important relationship. It is perhaps due to Gerda that my father went to a performance of the remarkable Josephine Baker, of whom I have a signed photograph. He told me that she was one of two black people he saw in his life before he arrived in America. The photograph dates from Baker's heyday in 1931.

Figure 2.4: My father's girlfriend Gerda Bauer, a dancer

Figure 2.5: Autographed postcard of Josephine Baker, 1931

It is much easier for me to recreate my father's perspective on society. He became a convinced, model working-class socialist who was uncomfortable with middle-class people while having a certain admiration for business successes. He believed in a state that protected workers from cradle to grave, organised pensions and health systems and housing, and made it difficult for workers to be fired. He was not much interested in liberal democracy and, following the formal position of Austrian social democrats of the time, had little against Communism, though Russia may have seemed a bit harsh and crude because of its historical backwardness. However, he would have had relatively little in common with liberal-inflected leftists interested in liberation movements, feminism, social experimentation and the like, as were so many of his contemporaries in Europe. On a positive note, he had, despite limited formal education, an intense appreciation of the need to understand foreign languages, history and politics; to educate himself.

The vector of this kind of politics, together with the intensified nationalism of his generation, led him to become a keen Zionist. His kind of Jewish nationalism can be characterised as forming in response to the anti-Jewish climate among German nationalists and had little to do with Jewish culture or religion. The religion was fine for the basic rites of passage but otherwise, he once told me, it was largely suitable for old ladies. He certainly was brought up to despise Hasidism and the religiosity and outward signs of Jewishness that typified so-called *Ostjuden* – Jews from the East – whose ways Christian central Europeans found alien and dark. Zionism was about returning to the land, eliminating religious and bourgeois cultural elements, and focusing on agriculture, working with your hands and military preparedness – the very things that German nationalism treasured. An unusual aspect that was distinctive about him was his respect and liking for the new lands of Czechoslovakia (he understood some Czech) and Yugoslavia and for his birthplace, Italy.

I can recall walking with my father through the streets of Mödling, as he pointed out to me individuals as they passed by, surmising from their gait and clothing whether they were likely to be decent socialists or detestable ex-Nazis. Mödling, perhaps because of its proximity to Vienna, had a fairly strong socialist element and was bitterly contested before 1934 between the Christian Socialists and the Social Democrats. A Nazi rally atop the Eichkogel hill in 1924 concluded with a march in town. For two hours, a riot reigned, in the course of which a Social Democratic town councillor was killed.[2] My father had very good relations with his neighbours across the fence, the very Austrian Guggenbergers (who are still there), and with the artist Hans Essinger, whom he knew from schooldays. Essinger was an anti-Nazi. Yet the political caricatures Carlo drew, generally about class, were rather gentle and intended to raise a laugh rather than a sneer. He loved drawing, and a few of his caricatures were published in newspapers. His father and brother also drew for pleasure but not with the same seriousness of intent, however much Carlo always insisted this was merely his hobby. In his art, he found himself. By the time of the Nazi annexation, the *Anschluss*, he had just turned thirty-six, no longer a young man.

My mother, by contrast, can be described more easily in a way because she typified the values of thousands of well-off Jewish families in pre-war Austria, whereas my father was somewhat unusual. There are some important hiatuses but it is equally true that I knew her far better and so have richer detail about her life as well. Liesl, as Elisabeth was always called, was born in 1912. She saw very little of her father as a small girl. He was first of all away in America and then in the army for the four years of war, during which time her mother moved in with her aunt and grandfather, to whom she was consequently very attached.

With the war over, the Gross family moved into the big apartment on the Fasholdgasse in Hietzing, the thirteenth district, which was considered a suburb of villas and comfortable homes. Liesl attended the *Mädchenreformrealgymnasium* (Girls' Reformed Secondary School) in the Wenzgasse. Founded in 1903, this was a girls' school with a reputation for taking academics seriously as opposed to the traditional finishing schools my grandmothers had attended. From 1921 on, the school accepted girls who wanted to take the academic final exam, the Matura. Two years later Liesl entered the school and graduated in 1931, when she started her studies at the University of Vienna. In her time many of the university students were Jewish. She began studying social work with an earnest intention to help poor people with problems. However, she abandoned this after some time and shifted to the humanities. Why she made this choice I cannot say; perhaps it was the fate after 1934 of the Jewish and socialist social workers, who were dismissed. There was an interest in politics and in socialist ideals that singled her out from most of her friends. This she would retain at heart in America. She took herself seriously, wrote poems and read extensively, primarily writers who fitted her own outlook. In May 1932 she received a qualification to teach English. She finished coursework in July 1935, submitted her thesis in 1936 on the longer poems of the American writer Edwin Arlington Robinson,[3] and finally graduated in May 1937, the last graduation before the arrival of Hitler. She also studied art history as a secondary subject with some focus on the early Renaissance.

How can one classify her interests retrospectively? It is striking that she had little attraction to the avant-garde. She liked nineteenth-century modernity and certainly admired English and American culture. Her book collection, which she later shipped to America, contained a lot of foreign authors, socialists and pacifist novelists. She owned books by English writers –George Bernard Shaw, John Galsworthy and H.G. Wells. She had a good understanding of classical music but it was very much the music of

Vienna from Haydn to Brahms. Yet her surviving archive of programmes of the concerts and operas she attended is a remarkable and cherishable record of the great performers of her day.

The professional idea behind her education was to become a teacher of English. Late in the day she discovered that under the Christian Social administration, Jewish girls were no longer hired to teach in Viennese schools. Thus in the last months of normality, she did a bit of tutoring and helped out in the family business while considering a future move. She was a mix of familial respectability and deference to high culture, and very recognisably a forerunner of the secular, holiday- and security-loving European middle-class culture post-1945. Her retention of essentially socialist ideas when it came to politics was anomalous; it was not shared by her American friends, certainly not the ones who also emigrated to the US, so it is difficult to know from where it came.

One thing that she definitely did not like at school was the compulsory lessons in Judaism. The Jewish girls were excused from Christian religious courses but a rabbi came to impart Jewish ways to them as a required extra subject. It gave her a lifelong distaste. Her little cousin Hella's father shared this dislike to the extent that he went to law to get his own daughter excused at the same school many years later. That my mother liked to tell me this suggests that she rather relished her uncle's efforts. She would share with my father this distaste as well, though she lacked entirely his interest in Zionism. The idea of a country just full of Jews had no appeal to her, she told me. However, she had unbounded admiration for an idealised image of the Jewish scientist, doctor or musician, or even entrepreneur, and more so if the individual was a female. This contradictory perspective seems odd at a distance, but in fact it was very typical of the time and place.

The holidays were numerous. She got bored in Bad Gastein despite the company of her sister Gerti and her much younger cousin Hella. But there were many excursions to the mountains and especially the lakes where swimming was popular. After school in the winter, it was possible to take one's skis on the streetcar up to a hillslope, and this she often did. She did not like wilderness or, indeed, animals, and she once told me that the best thing about hiking in the mountains was always the distant view of the village steeple far below – and the next best was the *Jause*, the Austrian version of the mid-morning snack.

Figure 2.6: Liesl and Gerti Gross with their friends Lenchen Dukes and Hella Censor, 1938

In 1935 or 1936 she made an adventurous organised student trip, partly by boat, to the nowadays popular coast of Croatia as far as Dubrovnik, a trip she always remembered fondly. After graduation, reward was a summer journey to Italy – the great artistic sites and then the Adriatic coast at Riccione, which Austrians still favour. In 1932 and again in 1935 she went to England, largely to research her thesis. On the second trip she stopped in Brussels and saw the World's Fair. She liked England very much. By contrast, she never returned after 1918 to Hungary (with one minor exception) or Czechoslovakia and had little identification with the family past. Among many cousins, she was friendly with only a few. The larger family interested her very little.

As an unmarried young woman in her twenties, the surviving correspondence and photos show a very strong attachment to a group of friends, of whom there is much evidence. All of them came from pretty much the same kind of background. There was Feri – Ferdinand Uprinny, my mother's boyfriend. The correspondence with Feri is slight but continued from 1929, before the end of schooldays, up to 1936, although it includes a card of congratulations on my mother's taking a degree. There is an interesting photo of Feri in what appears to be a socialist *Schutzbund* uniform. The Uprinnys seem to have sold watches and their address on the Pötzleindorfer Strasse in the 18th district, Döbling, suggests a wealthy home bordering some of the villas of the richest families in the city. Apparently at some point they made it clear that their son needed to make a more appropriate match and the understanding with Liesl was broken, probably in 1936. This was a kind of unhappy secret that was never revealed in any of my mother's innumerable intimate conversations with me during her lifetime; it was only after she died that my aunt told me the secret. It signals the extent to which, among the upper crust in this bit of an older Europe, marriages were still often expected to be advantageous rather than merely romantic.

It is intriguing that the surviving evidence suggests an interest in my mother on the part of men from very different backgrounds whom she

Figure 2.7: Feri Uprinny, my mother's boyfriend

met in her travels. There was a romantic photograph and postcard from an Italian chap she met in Riccione – Giorgio. There was clearly an interest from the young Englishman of the family with whom my mother boarded in Bromley, London. One can add an Indian student, presumably Muslim, from Amritsar, Mohibul Hasan. None of these men were Jewish or central European. On this account, the pleasant life of the Jewish bourgeoisie in Vienna, to a large degree socially cut off from the larger population, does suggest a kind of golden cage more than a golden age. These contacts hint at a potential break with Liesl's Viennese cake of custom, a break that in cultural terms could have happened but never really did. Yet while other men did appear in my mother's life, the rejection by Uprinny was a major blow, and the failure of Liesl's degree to lead to the start of a fixed career was another. Thus she was at a loose end when suddenly the tsunami struck.

3 | The Dark Years

Mounting pressure from Germany culminated in German troops cross-ing into Austria on 11 March 1938. By the 15th Hitler had reached Vienna in triumph and was ready to annex the *Ostmark* as just another German province. There remains controversy as to what the majority of Austrians really thought of this event: the virtually unanimous endorsing plebiscite was unlikely to have been accurate as a considered measure. However, nobody can doubt that many, probably most, Austrians saw the joining, the *Anschluss*, as an event that would give Austria a chance to revive economically and to thrive as part of a resurgent Germany. There were second thoughts about the loss of all sovereignty and, perhaps more so, the totally secular character of the new regime, which pushed aside Catholic institutions.

Yet many commentators noted the enthusiasm about attacks on Jews in Vienna, which went beyond anything arranged by the Nazi militants. Here was revenge against these arrogant, domineering people who had thought that they ruled the roost. Liesl's friend Hans Sorter wrote about his first experience in a letter years later. The office boy, who normally greeted him, in the MGM film offices where he worked, as Herr Sorter, with a dutiful salute, now announced on his arrival at the office one morning that Sorter was fired and he was in charge.

My parents recognised the difference between Nazi supporters and others, but they would certainly acknowledge that Vienna's new bosses were popular, more so as unemployment got mopped up and better times restored quite speedily. For my mother, her gut feeling was the sensation of being excluded from joining what was clearly a vast popular movement. My father also told me that the problem with Jews was that they were too massively and obviously successful. The nastiness that Jewish people experienced, perhaps not infrequently reflecting a hostility long present but usually carefully masked, was accompanied by some ruthless action on the part of the new state. Yet many violent and cruel deeds were actually spontaneous and not directed from the state. They fitted the new system.

This created a mood of agitation that went beyond anything in the previous five years in Germany and made young Jewish adults determined to leave the country, if need be with nothing. One possibility in the first weeks was to cross the Swiss border, where thousands gathered in camps and waited for papers that could take them further. One of those that left was Feri Uprinny.

And it was not only the privileged who left. Only five months after Hitler took power in Austria, Carlo wrote in August 1938 from Mödling, thinking of his own friends, that 'soon it will be very empty here'. His own brother, by chance, had been in Yugoslavia for work at the time of *Anschluss* and would stay out permanently. However, this was anything but easy to effect. According to Liesl, this was a time of fear and terror but also one of excitement and living by one's wits that defied the confines of normality and stretched ingenuity.

The two countries that head the list of destinations to which Austrian Jews fled between 1938, when Hitler arrived, and 1941, when the doors closed entirely, were the United Kingdom and the United States.[1] Although Britain tops the list, I shall focus here on the United States, because it was there that my parents ended up. The US was highly desirable as a new home, reflecting the European mythology of the Golden Land of the West where all comes right. However, the US imposed quotas reflecting late-nineteenth-century countries of origin on would-be immigrants. Would-be immigrants filled out the requisite forms with trepidation, fearing to be tripped up. The key to entrance was the affidavit, a mysterious word when I was a child, evoked so often but never used in the normal language of school and the commercial world. A resident American with reasonable resources had to vouch for the immigrant and promise to support him or her if all else failed. Thus, contact with friends or relatives in the US became a life-or-death matter. Even then, all was not certain. Breckenridge Long has become notorious as the key figure in the State Department who requested consuls to delay or block, if they could, desperate people who had all the legal papers. There were also many individuals, it must be said, some based in Europe, dedicated to bringing people to safety in the New World, especially those they knew personally.

It was certainly easier to get into the US before 1938, during the first five years of Nazi rule in Germany proper. Overall, probably a hundred thousand German Jews did settle in America, but the figure for Austria was less than thirty thousand in the first instance. My parents' stories in this regard are characteristic of the chances that enabled entrance to take place. In Carlo's case, we have to go back to earlier family history. The Freunds turned to the now middle-aged women, the cousins of my grandfather Wilhelm, whom he had helped a generation before to go to Chicago. The streets hadn't turned to gold for them. Neither Irma Davis in San Francisco nor Stella Chapman Lieberman in Chicago, as these two ladies were now called after a couple of marriages, had the wherewithal to help. However, they apparently turned to a relation, Frank Dusek, who had prospered in America, and he was willing and able to vouch for the Freund brothers.

In my mother's case there were two saviours whom my grandfather Josef Gross had befriended in the course of chatting to foreigners in his business premises. One was a courtly Hungarian, Aladar Hamburger, who was prepared to return to Vienna from Chicago and, in the end, to Trieste, to ensure all was in order to bring Josef to America. He certainly had to pester the consul, who belonged to the Long school of US hospitality. In addition, there was a one-time medical student in Vienna, now the successful Dr Perlstein, also by chance resident in Chicago. Nonetheless, it took considerably more time for my grandmother to get the nod than her daughters; and my grandfather, because of his chance birth in Lviv, had to be placed on the long lists that belonged to the Polish quota.

To understand the refugee experience, it may be useful to look in some detail at my parents' experiences. My mother and her sister Gerti were determined to emigrate from the start. At the time of the Munich crisis in the summer of 1938, their bags were packed and they were prepared to cross the Swiss border somehow. In fact, the crisis did pass momentarily and they soon afterwards secured their American visas. One way of using their Deutschmarks was to travel via Bremen on a German ship, the *Europa*, as though they were tourists. They made the mistake on one occasion of wearing the Austrian national costume, the *dirndl*. This was a kind of symbol of Austrian self-assertion and of Jews being legitimate Austrians, and was greeted with insulting behaviour on board, something that my mother told me she had not previously experienced. This violated the sense of normality that came with the tourist-like snapshots of the trip, which also survive.

Very soon after arriving in New York, terrible news arrived. So-called *Kristallnacht*, the night of the breaking of glass, which involved the physical destruction of virtually every synagogue in Germany and the territories it now occupied, as well as other Jewish institutions, was arranged as revenge for a Jewish boy assassinating a minor official in the Paris embassy, his response to the desperate state of his parents caught between being deported from Germany and being unwelcome in Poland. The Jewish community was now charged for all the insurance costs, Jewish businesses were shut down or confiscated, and Jewish civil rights dramatically curtailed. Thousands of able-bodied men were arrested and sent to concentration camps with the intention of scaring them into emigrating – anywhere.

Figure 3.1: Liesl and Gerti Gross aboard the *Europa*, September 1938, en route to New York

These were not death camps, but several hundred died nonetheless in the course of *Kristallnacht* and its aftermath, a shocking break with any 'modern' normality. Josef Gross was not one of those arrested; he fortunately got wind of what was happening and managed not to be at home when the police arrived. His great worry was that he would be deported to Poland 'comfortably even without a suitcase', as he put it, and knowing nobody.

In the early months of 1939, the correspondence was all about visas and affidavits and the arrangements for shipping household goods to the US, even brooms and irons. With the business closed down, the Grosses took the decision to live off the proceeds from selling the larger furniture and move into their daughter and son-in-law Steffi and Fritz Kornfeld's flat in the Doblhoffgasse, which had once belonged to Markus Munk. Josef kept his spirits up. He wrote in broken English that 'I am healthy and I am to make soon more money as you belief. I like to forget the German language!' He was then sixty-three. The contact with Chicago was a lifeline. In May they were just able to celebrate my grandmother Lucie's fiftieth birthday and enjoy the chocolate bonbons from Chicago – not, of course, as good as the Viennese varieties, now forbidden to Jews. They also took a long last walk on the Anninger just above my father's home town of Mödling, 'a proper, lovable Vienna Woods landscape replete with a view over vineyard-covered hills', as Lucie described it.[2]

Figure 3.2: My grandparents Josef and Lucie Gross, 1938

How did she feel? 'Here Life is becoming so unreal that sometimes you cannot believe that what is happening is true, then you lose yourself in fantasies, how things were, when the summons [to go] shall arrive. Then come days too, when one is overcome with anxiety from which there is no escape. In a word there are completely unnatural psychological circumstances and you need strong nerves to get through this time.' There was still work to do with her sister in winding up the business, but otherwise she focused on improving her sewing so that she could perhaps work with Gerti to establish a little business in Chicago (this actually came to pass) and she tried to improve her English. Josef assured my mother that 'Vienna is no more Vienna – it's becoming a faded provincial German town'. Provisions were scarce. Veal – for schnitzel – was not to be seen, and Jews were not allowed to buy fruit although butter was fortunately still available. Nonetheless, he wrote: 'We shall survive.' Of course, far worse was to come.

On 15 June 1939, however, Lucie was able to write that the *Vorladung*, a permit to enter the US, had arrived and she could make departure plans. Now it would be really and truly 'auf baldiges Wiedersehen'. 'Mir kommt es wie ein Traum vor, dass ich Euch bald wiedersehen soll, aber dieses Mal ist es ein schöner Traum. [It comes to me like a dream that I will soon see you again but this time it's a beautiful dream.]'

The next step would be a ticket for the journey by sea from Trieste in Italy. Josef planned to stay in Italy and await his visa in Naples. Indeed, he was still waiting for his name to come up on the US country list for Polish applicants. 'Onkel', that is to say Herr Hamburger, had explained to him that what he needed was a letter from his daughters to promise to support him while he stayed in Italy. Despite the first swingeing Italian laws aimed at Jews, this remained a real possibility at the time. The last household goods passed through customs in Hamburg and were shipped to the US. With Josef's precautions, most things got through; only the family silver was stolen by the authorities.

Then on 28 July 1939, Lucie wrote an extraordinary letter from Trieste. Already they felt free again. 'We have finally reached the Harbour and we feel safe.' The stalls were groaning with fresh fruit available to anyone who could pay, and Italian prices were very low. My grandfather wrote as well: 'God be praised that we are again *Mensch* [human beings] amongst *Menschen* ... wonderful.' He already had his permit to stay in Italy; the journey south had been without problems and 'now we can blur in memory those dramas and fearful experiences'. He felt that there was no need to proceed to Naples, but he would rather stay in Trieste, still a city (some twenty years after Italian occupation) with a strong Austrian cultural flavour. Lucie sailed to America in the last month of peace, on 3 August 1939.

Josef did indeed stay for many months in Trieste, although his chances of getting into the US improved with the extinction of Poland. Life in Italy was actually pleasant and his daughters' weekly $5 gift quite enough to live on in the circumstances. He had been suffering from gall bladder problems, but his health actually improved.

Finally, in the spring of 1940 his papers arrived in order. The US consul in Trieste was one of those who tried to limit immigrants and cause difficulties, but fortunately Aladar Hamburger was there to make sure Josef got on the boat. It was just after the Jewish holiday of Passover, which commemorates the crossing of the Red Sea. 'Here in Europe the sword of Damocles hangs over us and I am impatient' to leave, he wrote, but he could not refuse an invitation from Triestine Jews. 'Tonight I am an honoured guest at the first evening of Passover. I am also a guest for Easter: *"Ob ich will oder nicht, ich muss* [I must go whether I like it or not]."' How good these Italians are, he wrote, even though 'my great wish is to leave and join you'. This was the phase of World War II when Hitler was about to overrun Denmark and Norway; it was, indeed, very high time to leave.

My father Carlo's story is also worth telling. Awaiting some way out of Europe, he became more and more impatient in the summer of 1938 and he placed his savings in a Zionist organisation planning to smuggle emigrants illegally to Palestine. On this basis, he got himself a passport, issued on 29 September, and on 3 October he wrote a card to his mother from Aachen, close to the Dutch border. Shortly after that, he crossed illegally to Maastricht and then on to Belgium. However, he and others were rounded up in a Brussels café where their illegal papers were identified and they were sent home by train.

His brother was no longer at home. Rico had been on his usual rounds in Yugoslavia at the time of the *Anschluss* and contrived to stay out of the Reich, primarily in Bucharest, in Romania, where it was possible to bribe officials at least for a time. He felt desperate at being separated from Gabriele, his mother, but there was nothing more possible than a telephone call. A planned reunion in Budapest could not take place. Jews could normally not leave Germany and re-enter with the letter 'J' stamped on their passports.

Carlo was one of the victims of *Kristallnacht*, one of the Jewish men hauled off to Dachau, where he proceeded to spend seven months. Overworked and underfed, he lost weight drastically and was in terrible shape when he finally got out. The testimony of my uncle Artur Kerdemann, incarcerated for a time at Dachau with my father, mentions what I was always told: that he almost died.

As with her stepbrother Artur, it was Betty Zehner who went to the Gestapo headquarters to pick Carlo up; his mother couldn't bear to do it. By good luck the US visa had just come through and Carlo was free to leave for America. He had a short phase of recovery in the Rothschild Hospital, which still looked after Jewish people, and became attached to a nurse named Liesl Nassau, who was listed as deported to Theresienstadt, where she died in 1943. My father always kept a picture of her. On 22 August 1939 he left Austria for the sea journey and sailed from Trieste on 19 September.

Figure 3.3: Carlo Freund, July 1939, after seven months in Dachau

War had just been declared and a British ship forced the Italian *Vulcania* to turn in at Gibraltar, but as Italy remained neutral for the time being, the ship was allowed to continue to Lisbon and then New York, arriving there on 2 October 1939. His brother Rico's papers had come by this time and he also sailed for America, in his case to settle in San Francisco, two thousand miles from Chicago, where Carlo had landed.

Let us go back briefly to my grandmother Lucie Gross's first letter from Italy. When she comments on her final days in Vienna, the tone is sombre and she calls those days *aufregend*, crisis-ridden and upsetting. Her sister was being ordered to leave her flat for the Josefstadt district, like other Jews. The people she knew were depressed, frightened and impoverished, their normal lives already wrecked. In those days, she visited what she called the *eingeschmoltzen*, moulded-together, family. She would never see any of these people again and they all would be sent to terrible deaths 'in night and fog'. The exception was my great-grandmother's sister Netti. She had talked and talked the Gestapo out of making her move. She would never leave Vienna but would die in the city where she had made her life, early in 1942 at the age of 85 or 86. She is buried with her husband, who had died thirty years before, but there was no possibility of anyone carving her name next to his on the tombstone.

Figure 3.4: A last look at the dining room of my grandparents' home in Hietzing, Vienna, before leaving Austria

Figure 3.5: Carlo Freund's farewell to his mother, Gabriele, before his first attempt at flight (note his characteristically Austrian loden jacket)

Words are eloquent but sometimes one turns with profit to the visual. My mother photographed the apartment on the Fasholdgasse, the only home she had known, and took a snapshot of the Burgtheater festooned with swastikas. My father drew in detail the house on the Badstrasse and his room, when his health recovered. The photograph of his mother and himself dressed in the loden jacket so characteristic of Austria and southern Germany tells a tale. Most dramatic is a terrifying picture of roll call in Dachau.[3]

My own parents talked a great deal to me about their last days as Europeans under Nazi rule, but they never talked about or sought to learn about what happened to those who could not get away and were sent into this unforgiving hell. Inevitably I mean these pages to be a memorial to those who died.

Figure 3.6: 'Dachau: The Roll Call', by Carlo Freund

Let me start with two descriptions. On the Judenplatz in Vienna, the heart of the ghetto in the fourteenth and fifteenth centuries, a monument has been erected to the deported and killed, designed by the British sculptor Rachel Whiteread. It looks like a sealed-up library and it has the names of all the places to which transports were sent, an accurate account of the places to which relations of mine were dispatched. It's a fitting monument, which brings me to tears.

On the Web there is an alphabetical list available of all the people recorded as having been on those transports: more than forty thousand sent from Austria. This list is incomplete but it represents just under a third of all the people in Austria in 1938 classified as Jewish. This classification included individuals with only one or two Jewish grandparents, whatever their religion, and excluded converts to Judaism, a category reached largely as a result of intermarriage. I am struck by the ages of the people who were on the list. They were overwhelmingly, although far from exclusively, people in later middle age or elderly. Most younger adults made their escape. Those who stayed tended to be the poor, the elderly, the sickly and those who were simply reluctant to abandon their ordinary lives for an unknown future until it was too late.

On my father's side of the family, the most dramatic loss was my grandmother Gabriele. Past the middle of 1941 she was still in correspondence with her sons; she knew about their marriages and wrote to Liesl and to Lucie to introduce herself. She was living, no doubt, in very cramped and impoverished conditions – having had to make a forced sale of the little house in Mödling as my father was leaving Austria – on the Novaragasse in the Josefstadt along with thousands of other ghettoised people, with the hope of escape to America. Indeed, the papers submitted by my father and uncle to support her came through, but it was too late. There was no way to get to a boat, the Americans had closed their consulates in Germany, and Hitler and his entourage, once the invasion of Russia had begun, were determined to kill off the Jewish population under their control en masse. In January 1942, she was deported to the Latvian capital of Riga. Very few on that transport survived and she very likely died of privation on the long train journey or was shot on arrival. There is one account by a survivor of that transport or at least one of a number in that month. He reported that elderly people, including his own mother, were taken aside on arrival, and shot. In any case, Gabriele was never heard from again. She was sixty-seven years old.

On my mother's side of the family, the equivalent dramatic tragedy was the death of her aunt and uncle, Steffi and Fritz Kornfeld. They were reluctant to abandon life in Vienna, and this would be their downfall. By the time Josef and Lucie Gross left the Kornfelds' apartment in June 1939, the latter too had been served with notice to vacate. Fritz was an early victim of the regime. Records show that towards the end of the year he was sent to Nisko in Poland with perhaps a thousand others. This was a purported camp near the new armistice line with Russia in Poland, but nothing there was prepared and the local German authorities did not cooperate with this plan. Some of the men managed to escape across to Soviet lines and convince the authorities that they were not enemies of Communism but Fritz died in the winter in Nisko.

His adolescent daughter Helli could well have survived. She was given a place in an English boarding school through a *Kindertransport* initiative but, when she arrived at the airport, she and her mother Steffi could not bear to part from each other. This incident horrified the Gross sisters and their parents, and confirmed Josef's view that Steffi was a foolish woman in

Figure 3.7: Helli Kornfeld, my mother's cousin, as a thirteen-year-old, 1938

practical matters, a story I was often told growing up. She perhaps hoped her Yugoslav in-laws, who were able to visit, could help her, but this was not possible and they settled down to wait for the permission to travel to the US. But by this time the lists were extremely long and the wait was long too. Reading Helli's last penned lines in 1941 congratulating my mother on her marriage fills me with sadness. In April 1942 she and her mother were sent to Izbica, a small town in southern Poland that had once been mainly populated by Jews, now all murdered. Here, according to accounts, Jewish prisoners were either shot or sent fairly soon to the gas chambers at Belzec, where several hundred thousand died in a location on a railway siding intended for that purpose. Not a single individual on the Izbica transport with them is known to have survived.

4 | A New Life in America

I can only guess at my parents' state of mind when they came to Chicago. They met each other at a social event organised for single refugees like themselves. My father must have been very lonely; it is hard to know whom he could have spent time with or seen or how he lived for his first few years in America. My mother lived with her family but she watched her younger sister marry and her parents gradually age. I imagine that both she and my father were very eager by the spring of 1941 to find someone congenial with whom they could perhaps salvage a new life. They had in common – from Austria – the same taste in food, the same closeness to strangers who may have held different ideas, intimacy at home where polite manners were discarded, the same respect for high cultural institutions (and pre-scribed medicine), the same need for relaxation through vacations – two a year, for one of which I was hauled out of school for an extra week – an eccentric practice in America where vacations were mostly a luxury for the wealthy. My mother would get extremely anxious if the vacation weather did not cooperate with her plans. There was for her some sense of entitle-ment to a brief, carefree escape from Chicago apartment life.[1] My parents also shared more or less the same political values from the Austrian social-ist tradition[2] and the same indifference to many poorly understood aspects of American life, of how Americans do things. Very significantly, they used money in much the same way and placed a similar value on how to spend it. In the old snapshots, they amused themselves in similar ways at home in their youth – skiing, hiking, swimming. The *Bad* in Mödling, the site of swimming baths for the public, was unique as a setting for separate snap-shots in both their collections.

Figure 4.1: My parents, Carlo and Liesl, get married, Chicago City Hall, May 1941

Both also shared the same attitude to Jewishness. There was nothing 'wrong' with it – inevitably one's friends came from these origins – but the general view was that the traditional Jewish ways, barring a sense of humour and an impressive cleverness, were not very nice and were to be suppressed whenever a trait that was identifiably Jewish came out. ('Don't talk with your hands!) In this they were very different from the mindset of American Jews, with whom they rarely made friends and with whom they were not particularly comfortable beyond perhaps an aligned sense of domesticity.

But they were also strikingly different from each other. By contrast with the bond between my aunts and uncles, who had chosen each other, as it were – both sets had been engaged to each other in the old country and joined up again romantically in the New World – this was a very different

Figure 4.2: Carlo becomes an American (settler with rifle)

kind of partnership. My father was a good ten years older than my mother and almost a foot taller. He had the identity of a self-conscious Austrian working man imbued with a socialist culture. This was tied strongly into his sense of masculinity; he didn't approve of 'uppity' women who liked to spend their husbands' money. He also had a sense of distance from the educated, even more so than those who had made some money from a business. He was very stingy. I realised one day many years later that whenever we went out to a restaurant, he almost invariably ordered the cheapest item on the menu, whatever that might be. He never owned a credit card and never bought anything on credit. He hated most aspects of American consumerism. I remember on holidays how he loathed Las Vegas and Miami Beach; even the sight of billboards annoyed him. My father would never have struck anyone as being Jewish. The one important Jewish identification

Figure 4.3: Carlo play-acts with a Menominee headdress

for him was a secular, socialist but militarised Zionism. I am inclined to think it was a riposte to the German nationalism that his earliest cartoons celebrated during World War I and that in effect rejected him. This mirrors the mentality of Theodor Herzl (who was a Viennese journalist, after all) and other Zionist pioneer thinkers.

Most of the time, my father worked on the top floor of Marshall Field's department store where he altered ladies' fur coats, mainly in the off-season. I think he had learnt this craft in Austria. In the late 1950s he broke free for a bit and worked in a sheet metal shop where he had spent some years during World War II. That came to an end with a recession and he was able to get his old job back but it was no source of rejoicing. It brought to an end the one effort to change our family lifestyle, to buy a little suburban house, a project abandoned during this phase of unemployment, around the time when I started high school.

My father's job was not unionised and it paid less well than my mother's. We faithfully went to the most unpretentious part of the famous store to buy all of our clothes discounted. My treat was to go to (I think) the fifth floor and buy postage stamps for my collection, augmenting the exotic items I could find at home from the old letters. When my father turned 65, he asked for and got some extra work, but he was pushed hard, with little regard paid for those long years of service. Once his Austrian pension came through, he left with no regrets.

Like his father and his brother, my father drew and painted 'as a hobby'. But I think he was the most interesting of them, perhaps by far. He liked drawing caricatures, a few of which were published in Austrian newspapers and which I have donated to the Austrian Caricature Museum in Krems on the Danube. In the first years in America, he painted some tentative advertising hoardings which were very attractive but never bought. Then came a series of oils which depicted Chicago life as a kind of expressionist multi-racial slum. His caricatures of Latinos and blacks are striking, unflattering but full of an unvarnished fantasy sensuality depicted by this obviously fascinated respectable working man. From the mid-1950s people started to disappear entirely from his work. Instead he painted watercolours set in Lincoln Park as well as scenes from our vacations. Here, Nature took over

Figure 4.4: Carlo (left) at a coffee break at his work, Marshall Field department store, Chicago

and the park became a surrogate for the kind of countryside he had loved in Austria.

None of this made the least bit of sense in post-war America. My father had no interest whatsoever in abstract expressionism or what followed, and his art reflected a sensibility from his own lost world. But it was an important hobby for him. This is what he worked on all weekend, sketching in the park in later years after appropriating my bicycle and then painting at home. In his last years, he taught a sketch class for elderly people, but his social interests were really very limited. He lived in himself and usually kept his thoughts to himself as well. I think his ego was so wrapped up in his drawing and painting that, although I have some ability and more imagination in this area (as opposed, say, to music), I would never have infringed on his territory by making the least commitment to this kind of expression.

Figure 4.5: Tawdry but sexy: a painting by Carlo Freund, 1959

Soon after coming to Chicago, the family benefactor, Dr Perlstein, used his influence with Morris Fishbein, president of the American Medical Association, to get a job for my mother at the Association's *Index Medicus*, a research journal which existed until its merger with an equivalent produced by the National Institutes of Health. My mother could then have moved to Washington to carry on, but this was out of the question. She translated German articles and edited them. This she liked very much; it fitted her sense of the beneficent role of doctors as the high priests of medicine. Dr Fishbein had his virtues and was an effective enemy of what he considered quack treatments such as chiropody, no doubt, but he is largely remembered today for his role in covering up the link between smoking and cancer.

By contrast with my father, my mother, although always happy to save money too, was not especially stingy. As a university graduate, she would have been a *Frau Doktor*, a cognomen she never used in America. She put great stock in the world of culture – literature, art, science and, being Viennese, classical music as the ultimate, whereas my father was happiest listening to oompah music and enjoyed a military band or a waltz. Her proclivities were those of a déclassée bourgeoise. I suspect that as a young woman she was more open to the avant-garde, but in my time she was, above all, attracted to stories of bourgeois women in crisis, so typical of nineteenth-century Europe – Ibsen, Flaubert, Tolstoy, Butler and many more. She admired career women. Perhaps in Vienna she might have become a secondary schoolteacher married to a successful and well-heeled professional man.

Figure 4.6: My mother in her fox jacket with American Medical Association office staff, c.1950

She was also very attached to her parents, her sister and to me, her one child who came forth after two miscarriages past the age of thirty. My father, as I have written, kept his thoughts to himself; he was extremely laconic and never discussed what he did during the day or much else. My mother, by contrast, liked her work and talked fascinatedly about the 'girls' with whom she spent her day. Her closest friends had a striking element in common with her – Minnie was the daughter of a Finnish rabbi in Cleveland who had been called to America from Helsinki and had an encyclopaedic knowledge of languages, a slightly rough-and-ready husband, and a daughter who was stagestruck; Fay came from a central German city after a couple of difficult years in Palestine with a son my age who also aimed at being an historian and eventually left America for Britain; Magda was the product of a family from the Hungarian gentry, born in Zagreb, with a daughter who had married a Jewish doctor, and got out of Hungary in 1956. Yet my mother also made friends with others of varied descriptions – Brazilian, Indian, Japanese – and greatly admired the women in charge of her office. Miss F had a permanent lover, legitimated owing to a husband with serious health problems. Mrs H, who was in charge of a specialised library at the University of Chicago, got a substantial promotion around 1970 and left the city and, with it, her husband. My mother got Mrs H's position in the course of trying to do a master's degree in library science, which she never achieved. It was not a very interesting job, but it meant in time automatic fee remission for me and the company was pleasant.

As it became affordable, my mother went to more and more concerts. Her tastes were pretty much confined to the epoch between Haydn and Brahms. She was not very interested in Bach or in Mahler. These tastes were very decided and changed little. She gradually lost her interest in literature, of which I think the most intense part involved writers with a pacifist, feminist and socialist background: Wassermann, Werfel, Zweig, Remarque. I don't think much literature of my time, whether American or European, spoke to her although she enjoyed Günter Grass.

My mother was very happy to discard the pretensions belonging to the milieu in which she grew up. She fussed very little about her appearance, she hated domestic chores (she would have loved to have a cleaning woman) and she was delighted that the 'girls' at the office would call her by her first name. Admittedly Liesl became Lisa, but that was OK. She also didn't mind living in small walk-up apartments. But in the end her tastes were very unlike those of my father, and I remember her pointedly telling me after the return trip to Austria finally happened that they could never have lived together in their home country.

The old snapshots show a physicality in their relationship from the early days, but whatever the cause and however this transpired, I have no memory of any physical contact between them. Indeed, as a boy I didn't often hear them talking to each other at all except to express some or other preference for what to watch on television or the like. I would get embarrassed as a boy when on hot nights my parents, notably my mother, hardly wore clothes. Romance didn't exist for me as a home feature except as a source of ridicule.

In the first years in Chicago, my mother and aunt befriended a little crowd of Viennese émigrés like themselves from similar class backgrounds. Some, though not all, of these wanted to break any formal link to Jewishness, so their children would no longer be troubled by this stain. In the course of ten to fifteen years, this group, or at least those with younger children living as families, left the city for suburbia. This was hardly going to be an easy move for my parents once they found each other. Then there was a more lower-middle-class or working-class crowd who suited my parents passably, much slower to advance to suburbia; they were the regulars among the family friends, the people that we used to meet at a familiar spot on Montrose Avenue beach in the summer among so many other little ethnic crowds.

Every other weekend on Sunday we headed up to the North Shore, to Winnetka, where my mother's sister and her husband, Gerti and Hans, had bought an old pre-World War I house, which accommodated my grandparents as well. Here in some measure the family core from Hietzing in Vienna was recreated. It was, I imagine, a sometimes comfortable and sometimes irritating destination for my father. We usually brought over as well my uncle's widowed mother, who always stayed in Chicago. Aunt Fritzi was a grande dame and, though her censorious power caused great friction with others, she brought charm and grandmotherly beneficence to my life, poor as she was. I liked going up to Winnetka very much. I can never forget the pleasure in summer of seeing my grandmother sitting on a rocking chair within an enclosed porch in front and waiting for our arrival.

The existence of this household owed a lot to the forceful, if at first gauche, personality of my very sociable aunt. Gerti had gone for one of her sister's friends, eight years older than herself, and made the commitment to him in Vienna. He and his brother – Hans and Ernst Frankl – were the potential heirs to a successful international agribusiness that reflected the family links with Hungary (where Fritzi had been born) and with what is today Slovakia (where Fritzi's husband came from), but neither son was an enthusiastic businessman. Ernst ultimately had a successful career as senior tutor at Trinity Hall, Cambridge.

Hans, the other brother, was an immigrant who never settled very well in America. After his time in the army, he used the GI Bill to acquire some kind of qualification as a bookkeeper, and that is how he spent his working life. He was a man who had loved the Austrian countryside, learnt fluent French and English, and was never so happy as when he was making puns or recalling favourite symphony performances – a highly intelligent man in his own way. His correspondence with Gerti from occupied Germany in 1945 is a revelation as regards his perfect English and his acute observations, but he was not an American business notable in the making. Like my own father, when he retired, he seemed, once he had made the proper gestures to everyone, to live very much in his own head with a minimum of communication, especially with the younger generation.

When in 1954 the Franklins, as the Frankls had become, abandoned Hyde Park, where they had first settled in Chicago after coming from Vienna, the trip up to the North Shore became a determinant feature of our life. (There were also a few joint holidays.) My grandfather Josef Gross was, in my childish eyes, a man with poor eyesight and only a moderate command of English. My cousins claim that even living with him they never saw him without his bow tie and relatively formal clothing. He was a distant figure who offered me half-dollars and postage stamps for my collection. The only one of his siblings (I believe) to have remained Jewish, he was pleased that the Freunds at least went through the conventional motions of a bar mitzvah and Jewish adherence. In Vienna he had liked going to the lovely Biedermeier synagogue in the centre, the first constructed in the modern city, for High Holy Days, but on his own. He died a few years after the move to the North Shore. I loved my grandmother to bits and still miss her. She was the storybook grandmother who loved me, listened to me, and took an interest in whatever I told her. She was still a talented pianist, having once been a very good one, and she was also a prize-winning cook.

But I enjoyed my cousins James and Richard too. They had, indeed still have, some of the virtues of the old country; they speak German, but they learnt to fit very well into the upper-middle-class WASP world surrounding them in Winnetka. My aunt, by promoting this move, made sure that they attended one of the most prestigious state schools in America. She also made sure that we went outside to get fresh air and played in all kinds of weather, that we hardly knew what a store-bought sweet tasted like (my grandmother could confect all the famous Viennese favourites), that my older cousin didn't waste his time on a sports team and that he grasped that his very substantial musical talent needed to be diverted into the world of hobbies, with no possible turn-off into Bohemia. This led to considerable worldly success.

Figure 4.7: My grandmother Lucie Gross playing the piano at the end of her life, with my cousin Richard looking on, in the Winnetka dining room, 1970

I can't say that Gerti was not a loving and kindly aunt, but she laid down a sort of ideology that had little place for my political ideas or for my intellectual bent. The good life meant a small family living around the proverbial corner and a family head who made good money in the business world, and I think in retrospect that this view was pretty much what sat in my mother's head. And it is not that I was not much attracted to the apparently bland and non-conflictual world of affluence I saw as a boy in Winnetka.

Our slow progression home south through the suburbs and then our coming at last into the city limits was usually a sad one for me. I still think of the city as a place of sidewalks lined with dirty sleet, dead pigeons filling the park underpasses, and brick buildings with unpainted sides like underwear showing.[3] I yearned for what Chicagoans call a 'yard' and the sense of a detached household where one could own a piano or keep a pet.

When I think about all those Chicago Viennese, few had any very clear grasp of US politics or any idea of an alternative to the dominant existing patterns. Yet my parents were most exceptional; throughout my years living with them they remained pretty faithful to Austrian social democratic ideas. They were both very pleased that the US entered the war and fought against Hitler. They would also have been keen on the left end of the New Deal: the beginning of pensions, public housing, public support for the arts and so on. The last president who had any appeal for them was Harry Truman, and they bemoaned the political failure of Governor Adlai Stevenson, a witty, cultured man and loyal Democrat, in his runs for president against General Eisenhower. As for Jack Kennedy, their long memory included an image of his father as ambassador to London with his known opposition to a war with Hitler, and the family's Catholicism was also not a recommendation. I remember as a boy watching TV with all of us glued to the Army–McCarthy hearings. I certainly identified with the Rosenberg boys whose parents were legally executed. Even in retrospect now, taking action then so the Russians would have the bomb and not be victims of US aggression makes sense to me, treason in a higher and nobler cause, although apparently the Rosenbergs gave away little or nothing of value themselves. My parents must have been transfixed and horrified by the Red Scare years; it certainly meant that they kept their ideas within our four walls. I also remember that in 1959, when after many years of trying the White Sox won the baseball pennant, my parents were outraged that the city alarm bells, meant to announce a possible nuclear attack, were instead used to celebrate something so juvenile and unimportant.

My mother, no doubt influenced by her workmates, would gradually evolve into more or less a US liberal, with a declining interest in foreign affairs. She voted for Illinois' first black senator, a woman, for instance, and was willing to stand aside from typical US white prejudices as she got used to working with black people. My father, who had a very strong sense of working-class masculinity, wanted very much to identify with white working-class Chicago men in this regard and became obsessed with blacks bringing crime and grime to the city. In the hope of putting them in their place, he ended up supporting Ronald Reagan. He found Reagan's anti-Communism idiotic, but foreign issues by the 1980s did not matter so much to him. It was noticeable to me that when a black voice came on the television, the remote would click, the only exception being the case of a newscaster.[4] Neither of my parents had any time for the cultural shifts of the 1960s and afterwards.

As a little boy, I was small, thin, awkward, physically timid and book-ish, but also wilful and articulate. I was one of those children who banged their heads against the wall when frustrated. When I was still under the age of three, I walked along the raised concrete enclosure of a sandlot in Lincoln Park less than a foot high and fell off, breaking my leg. I had the presence of mind even then to tell my mother repeatedly that the leg had been broken, and indeed it was. I loved going to the Belmont Street library and listening to Mrs Barlow read children's literature on Saturday mornings. I treasured the few books that I owned, a mix of many of the best-known classics from different countries; indeed, I still remem-ber most of them. Paris meant Babar, London meant Mary Poppins, England as a whole was the domain of the little creatures in *The Wind in the Willows*, Italy meant Pinocchio, Copenhagen meant the little mermaid and the match girl, and Russia meant Peter and the Wolf. I did have a few American favourites too and the grim Brothers Grimm ensnared me into the German-speaking world. My mother recalled that once I began school as a six-year-old and reading was part of the curriculum, I picked it up very rapidly, and quickly acquired a huge vocabulary. When I started to be the one reading the books out loud, my parents demurred and let me get on with what I have done ever since my whole life long.

Chicago did not seem to my parents an attractive city to look at, given its harsh climate and our location in a walk-up red-brick apartment. However, they did much appreciate the civic culture, which provided a number of impressive free museums, a good public library system, a wonderful Art Institute that was also free, many parks and public beaches, the Lincoln Park Zoo and adjoining conservatory. With time their values would alter somewhat, but only after I left home.

When I was growing up, the North Side of Chicago was the home par excellence of the children and grandchildren of European immigrants. In an area that was flat as a pancake with straight streets that stretched for miles and miles, the most typical form of housing was the walk-up apartment in a six-apartment building. For the most part these apartments were decent enough for small families. A long corridor connected the living room, with the television set the pièce de resistance (we acquired one very early, in 1949), and the dining room at the back. The one remarkable feature was the border of Lake Michigan, which gradually swept slightly to the west as the shore reached north. Here was extensive park coverage and several beaches, crowded with thousands during the short, humid, hot summers.

Beside the park was Lake Shore Drive, where traffic could sweep up between downtown and the northern suburbs. In our neighbourhood, Lake View, there were numerous high-rises along the drive, some with beautiful old apartments built during the Roaring Twenties and others added from the early 1950s. To the west, the side streets also at first held very nice apartment blocks, but the quality became more modest as the long block ended and reached Broadway, where my primary school was situated. Then west of Broadway, where we lived, came more buildings housing respectable working-class and lower-middle-class families, with some poorer-quality housing along the transport-heavy business streets such as Broadway, Clark or Halsted.

Harvey Zorbaugh's classic *The Gold Coast and the Slum* was a sociological hallmark written at the end of the 1920s about the North Side, though a bit further south, nearer to the city centre. Here were the grandest apartment buildings of all as well as hotels such as the Ambassador East and the

Figure 4.8: Belmont Avenue Station, Chicago

Drake. But, generally speaking, at least until the 1960s the real Gold Coast excluded Jewish tenants through so-called restrictive covenants, which only then became illegal. Before that, Jews looked further north, those with money who were not taken by the idea of suburban living staying near to Lake Shore Drive, while other families left the old West Side tenements for the Lake View area but further back from the lake. Right in the middle of my primary school district, facing the Drive and the park, was the grandiose Temple Sholom. This mix – so different from east to west – was what I grew up with, and from it I learnt what class meant.

It is a not very original observation that Jewish immigrants and their descendants were delighted with the American system whereby all religious reference was excluded from the state schools. In my time, our little patriotic Pledge of Allegiance to the flag was cut so that even the words 'under God' were excised. On this basis, Jews had no interest in creating a separate school system and used the public schools en masse. In the 1950s only a forward minority of Jewish families bought houses in suburbs which maintained their own school district systems. The majority continued to use the Chicago public schools, part of a large and pretty uniform system with unionised teachers and administrators relatively newly emancipated from political appointments. There was, additionally, a large parochial school system for Catholics, dependent on the cheap labour of priests and nuns, where schools were single-sex, children wore uniforms, and discipline was reputedly strict. Though there were very few secular private schools in the city, I went to one as a little boy before I turned six, called Bateman School in the old Gold Coast, which I liked very much. It was close to the American Medical Association building, where my mother worked, and much of her salary went on sending me there so that she could work and get out of the house.

The North Side was heavily white with only a very few small segregated black pockets of little consequence. As the ghetto spread, the school district fathers would alter the boundaries after World War II so that whites could avoid the indignity of racial mixing. My own first experience of black people was with the Bateman driver, Booker, whom I got to know as a four-year-old and liked very much. It was a long time before a second black person came along in my life. The one significant though small presence outside the white spectrum was the group of Japanese-descended children, typically born in the Western concentration camps to which they were forcibly removed from the Pacific Coast during World War II. Some did not want to return to the Coast and reconstructed their lives instead in Chicago. Their values were the closest to those found in Jewish families but with some remarkable differences. I made friends among them and have always had a kind of attraction to Japanese style and culture ever since.

The schools in Chicago were very large. There were three large classes of forty-plus children for every year in my primary school. The fifty high schools all had enrolments in the thousands and my high school would hold more than three thousand at a time. The schools were in rather dreary and dirty brick buildings, the oldest part of mine having been erected in the 1890s. In primary school, we had just a gravel school yard. The only greenery was a narrow verge.

When apartheid ended and the anti-apartheid forces campaigned in the first election in 1994 for a Reconstruction and Development Programme, there was indignation that black South African children were forced into classes of over forty. I thought this an interesting figure, as we had usually a bit over that number in Chicago. My own conviction is that the character of a school is heavily dependent on the social character of the neighbour-hood and the intake more than on the quality of what is on offer. This is to distinguish between intellectual stimulation and mere order and discipline. Primary school (up to fourteen years of age) held virtually no extracurricu-lar activities. Classes, where individuals recited in turn, could be extremely boring, and I often whiled away the time by systematically reading the encyclopaedias lined up against the wall. Our teachers, invariably Jewish women (for whom this was still the most obvious respectable profession available on a big scale), varied in quality, not to say entertainment level. I have to remember Mrs Zelda Aronson, who took us for three straight semesters. She was very dull but kind enough to give me her old and (to me) fascinating pre-war copies of *National Geographic* as a gift. She was a tiny woman, and I remember being struck when, slight as I was, I actually reached and surpassed her height at about the age of eleven. Several of the teachers clearly thought I was very bright and were impressed while others disliked me because I did not fit in.

Intellectually, by far the most important influence was the final-year teacher, Sylvia Bloom. By chance, I knew her better than most because her son David, later a professional flautist with symphony orchestras in New Zealand and Australia, was just my age and because the Blooms became neighbours when we moved down the block from them. The Blooms were crypto-Communists, something I found congenial if exotic and fasci-nating. One remarkable result was that she exposed us to a unit in black American history. Interesting but intimidating was a mixer or two with students from a South Side high school, students who were much more physically developed than we were. Assigned a paper or two, I devoured books on black US history and culture, a hitherto unknown arena, for all my voracious reading thus far.

And what was I like? At the age we normally regard as the beginning of adolescence, my tastes changed radically. I remember taking a long walk through the park with my friend Peter Weil and realising that walking was great and Nature was great, not just something my parents favoured. I discovered classical music and started to be able to identify periods and composers. With a field trip to the Art Institute to visit a Picasso retrospec-tive at thirteen, I started to see how one could talk about modern art as more than just a matter of an individual's personal taste. The Art Institute became a place of real marvels for me; there was not much in it that I didn't love. I could not read enough history and was happy to make my way through literary classics albeit with imperfect understanding at times. As a boy I lived a great deal in my own head. I loved maps and atlases and had a repertoire of invented places and times. I had no problems with solitude. At twelve or thirteen I started to leave this behind for something more like the real world, but it was just a real world of books and schoolwork plus a social world of my friends.

5 | Adolescence: First Bridge to a Wider World

Adolescence is, of course, the time when you discover sex. The remarkable thing is that I didn't. A very sharp memory of mine concerns my second-grade teacher, Mrs Kauffman, who didn't much like me. I remember the little girls running about and giggling that Shirley Kauffman was going to have a baby. Clever as I was, I had no idea what they were talking about. How was this possible? I was fascinated that they could know such a thing. I no longer believed that babies were delivered by storks or were for sale at the department store, but I had also just never taken any interest in such matters. Then years later my mother gave me booklets that explained clinically what sex was and how babies were made. It sounded like a little operation in the hospital. I was astonished and laughed at myself: so that's how they knew. But I can't say this sex sounded like fun.

A big internal shift in me at this age did concern gender. Up to this point, my poor relations with my father and my close relations with my mother had led me primarily to identify myself with females. Now this changed, although I remained very timid and intimidated by anything that sniffed like machismo. In my secret imagination, I was the conquering hero. I didn't get on better with my father, worse if anything, but in fact the distance from my mother grew and in particular I confided less and less in her. This coincided with the shift to high school.

The break between elementary school and high school was a big one. The old Chicago school system lacked junior high schools. You remained in elementary school for eight years although there was some specialisation

BILL FREUND

in the final year. Then at age thirteen to fourteen, you progressed to a large public high school. In my case, this was in the year 1958.

Months before, the Russians had sent a satellite into orbit – *Sputnik*. This caused a panic in a wide array of US circles. What if American science lost its lead? What about the slack, relaxed way school teaching progressed in all too many schools? By this point in time, US schools were being subjected to considerable 'objective' testing procedures intended to determine our learning capacity. On one memorable such test, I had the highest marks, in a classroom of forty or more, for both verbal and mathematical ability and the lowest mark for mechanical ability. I did feel a bit of a freak. At thirteen I could distinguish between left and right only with difficulty, and I remember finding it hard to identify which bird wing was which in a drawing, as we were requested to do.

America was not, however, looking primarily for mechanical talent, and with my otherwise top scores I was admitted to a special programme called the 100s. A class of about twenty-five was selected for each of four years; given that our high school, Lake View, had more than three thousand students, I was part of a top tier of five per cent or less of the total class. There was a second, equally thin level called the Honours tier. This meant a shift for me from sitting in a class of forty listening to the weakest students in turn stumbling over the reading for the day, which was incalculably boring, to a life where henceforth I spent my time largely among a very small, select group indeed. Our five courses, counting the foreign language option, took up six of nine periods in the day, the rest being given to science labs. My life in high school was thus largely bounded by the 100s and the people within it. With a few minor hiccups, this was a pleasant and predictable reality.

In several respects, the Lake View catchment area was distinctive, stretching over a mile or more of lakefront, including smart Lake Shore Drive, and then perhaps two miles inland. A little outside this zone was Lane Technical High School, an all-male school yet much larger than ours and with a great catchment area covering the whole north side, reaching out to the skilled Chicago working class. Lane took in many of the boys who might otherwise have been assigned to Lake View, and one result was that our student body was no more than a third male. By and large, the whole Chicago public school system, attended by the great majority growing up in the city, was oriented first and foremost to building up this working class with American values and useful skills. I remember our physics teacher constantly urging the charms of DeVry Technical Institute as the place for boys to go after high school.

Apart from the handful of Asians and a few Latinos, whom we were used to regarding as just another ethnic group, not another race, this was a white student body. There were also a very few blacks but they belonged to a special little division for the deaf or severely hard-of-hearing and formed a tiny presence. The Chicago high schools were structured so that segregation prevailed despite the law. Every once in a while, the school boundaries were shifted so as to keep the races very largely apart. The North Side was in particular the preserve of the descendants of German and Scandinavian immigrants although there was a Jewish swathe that had begun on the old West Side and cut north. In the 1950s, after thirty years of severe immigration restriction, it was mainly among the elderly that you heard those strong guttural accents. Typically, the children I knew, unlike me, had only distant foreign roots, usually distilled through religious affiliation, and they were often confused about where their families had originated. The Jewish children certainly fitted this paradigm. They usually had only a vague idea of where in eastern Europe the trip to America had begun; ties had mostly been broken off by the time of the Holocaust, and the general view was that the pre-American past constituted the bad old days.[1]

The generation born in America was very adept at bettering themselves and began to discover the charms of affluence in the post-war years, if not before. Some twenty per cent of Lake View's graduates were Jewish. In my 100s class, these two characteristics were marked. The majority were Jewish and three-quarters of the classmates were female. In fact, there was considerable continuity from my primary school alone. Some of these individuals were very bright indeed, and they included the little nerdish group of boys with whom I proceeded to spend most of my days.

While the divisions weren't absolute, there was a spectrum that ranged from the poorer and intellectually hungrier to the more affluent and complacent among the Jewish group at large. My closest friend, Stuart Lasine, was the grandson of a pioneer psychiatrist and writer on Jewish culture who had a home library that impressed me. However, his mother had been a schoolteacher and his father drove a truck for his family's horse-radish business. Lenny was one of four children, the son of a postman and a Czech-born beautician. Michael's parents had come to Chicago from

Dublin (there was actually a little group of Irish Jewish immigrants with whom they socialised), the father a factory foreman and the mother a primary school physical education teacher. Jeff was the one exception: the son of a rather overbearing doctor. All of these boys eventually got PhDs although only Stuart and Michael carried on to life careers as academics. In fact, there were to be two other men as well as four women PhDs out of my high school graduating class of some three hundred and sixty. Stuart got his PhD from the University of Wisconsin in comparative religion and ended up teaching religious studies. He is the author of a few books, notably *Knowing Kings: Knowledge, Power and Narcissism in the Hebrew Bible*, in which he put his command of literary studies and lifelong fascination with psychology to work on the Old Testament. The other academic author from my year at Lake View High School, Beth Genné, studied art history and became an historian of dance. I knew her from my earliest childhood when we played together in Lincoln Park. Her very nice mother, another former crypto-Communist and later an activist liberal, was my favourite parent and was to some extent compatible with mine. Beth opened me up to the world of the arts as an adolescent, and even before, with her unique ability to connect different art forms. I think it has been a feature of my life, especially my earlier life, that I have been thrown together with and learnt from very smart individuals with very different kinds of interests from my own.

One of many curious coincidences in my life was the discovery of the Judaica library at the University of Cape Town many years later. The basis of this library was purchased from a family in Chicago whose intellectual daughter, Sara Duker,[2] was in the high school class the year after mine. I had seen that library once at a party in about 1962 and been quite awed by it. It made a lasting impression on me and it was astonishing to see it again on the slopes of Table Mountain forty years later.

As I recall, the group that came together was partly self-selected. Several boys who were invited to join in 1958 dropped out: they obviously did not want to exhibit a nerd badge in their high school world. Those of us who stayed were all too weedy and small to be plausible members of any school sports teams. While there were inevitably tensions at times, for me this was a comfortable and reassuring little community which I got very used to indeed. I remember it largely as a very pleasant time of life.

Stuart claims to have little memory of our teenage years. But what he does have is a kind of Kafka-like sense of disasters and humiliations. Objectively he was so respected for his wit and intelligence that it is hard to imagine that he held this self-image, but I suppose he did. He likes to harp on one short phase when we Jewish boys from the 100s were collectively bullied by the burlier guys from the regular classes for a few days at gym, the one class where we had to mingle with the hoi polloi. I think I may have got off more lightly than he did, but while he remembers this as a kind of brief reprise of the Holocaust, my only memory is of the chap who defended us without knowing any of us more than slightly. I could summon up a few other memories along these lines from primary school, but they were very few and far between. The most unpleasant I can recall relates to my being sent to a Jewish day camp in Michigan. Here I experienced some bullying and, in what was a good sign of my wilfulness, I demanded to be sent home – and was. It didn't endear me to more conventional Jewish male culture; I still remember being obliged to drink what they called 'bug juice' with meals rather than milk, in accordance with Jewish kosher strictures about mixing meat and milk dishes. I found this disgusting. At most, this kind of experience taught me to keep a distance from those unlikely to take to me and it enforced the solitary side of my nature. High school fitted this lesson very well.

When I think about those who in short order left this class, it may be interesting to mention the case of Wally Johnson. Wally had slicked-back blond hair and he looked like any ordinary working-class Chicago boy of the time. He was one of the boys who tested well, was placed in the 100s but quickly dropped out, which is why I knew him. But something happened to him that stuck in my memory: his older brother was killed by a policeman in an incident that was seen by Wally and others as a terrible travesty of justice. This gave me a disquieting sense of the police. They were certainly corrupt in Chicago and gave traffic tickets in order to meet their quota, but here was a story which suggested they policed not just race but occasionally class boundaries as well. Middle-class boys whose hair was not slicked back did not have this kind of thing happening to them, though there was a chance that they might get shaken down, as I once was.

Chicago was the site of the famous Daley political machine, a one-party state oozing patronage, and it wasn't a democracy in the way the enlightened, progressive middle class saw things. It hardly fitted what mainstream political scientists said DEEmocracy should be like. While this seemed wrong to me, I was also very aware of how comfortable and natural this seemed to my father. It can indeed be interpreted as consonant with socialism, as I have seen it interpreted in South Africa. As I came more to terms with my father's values, and also from many things I saw and heard in Chicago, I learnt about working-class life in a way that was very different from the liberal norms in much of genteel suburbia. I have long since shared his cynicism about that gentility which I much admired as a mid-teen but thereafter less and less.

In the middle of our four years of high school (1958–1962), things changed substantially as a result of the addition of several linkages. This meant the expansion of social life to include a number of the Honours class and notably graduates of the other catchment elementary school that bordered the lake. I took up with Lew Harris, a sunny, music-loving character, and Stu Schwartz. Both Lew and Stu have been very successful in the media world. Lew was a founder of the *Los Angeles Magazine* and pioneer of online journalism on the West Coast, and Stu became an American Broadcasting Company (ABC) executive; he's the father of the yet more famous newscaster Dana Bash in charge of CNN News today. I have to say somewhat shamefully that this expansion of my circle led to the peaceful extrusion of less intellectual and non-Jewish members, whom I would have described as less interesting as well. I should, however, mention the Hoerburger sisters. They were the daughters of a German immigrant milkman and his Jewish wife, who fell in love while singing in a choir. The parents shrewdly decided to help organise this young group into a pleasant but very innocent round of socialising, often to do with music, which provided us with many entertaining weekend events. As a whole, the range of friends I now had, which would not be duplicated in size or intensity for many decades, gave me a fairly rich social integument.

This crowd of friends was not entirely Jewish but it was largely so. I enjoyed Hebrew and Sunday School lessons and learning about Jewishness, up to a point. I went through a bar mitzvah at a little later than the average age, but I have to admit that by this time, at fourteen, I had lost my sense that Jewishness was something to believe in, much as I enjoyed performing before a crowd and receiving my premier gift, an *Encyclopaedia Britannica.* On the one hand, I was entirely comfortable with Jewishness in the sense of gesture, sense of humour and the like, and there was plenty to explore in the world of books, music and light entertainment to reinforce this. However, I also started to find this ghost of a 'way of life' confining, clearly the survival of something that had more intensity and more purpose in days gone by, and I started to look forward to exploring a wider world one day.

My parents never arranged for us to have a piano in the house although my mother as a middle-class Viennese girl knew how to play. My suburban cousins were exposed to the piano and Jim, the older boy, was a very talented and technically accomplished musician, playing the oboe in the school orchestra. I much regret that I never learnt to play an instrument. I did sing in choirs but stopped in college. I still have a taste for choral music and I am a systematic opera and symphony goer.

Lew, also a great music lover, led me in a different direction to the Old Town School of Folk Music. Folk music was a great accompaniment to an alternative sense of society and culture. I was entranced by the wonderful radio programme that filled so many Saturday nights, the *Midnight Special.* Another regular on WFMT radio was Studs Terkel. In my final year of elementary school he talked to us about jazz, and years later I much enjoyed his distinctive popular social history books. Gradually I emancipated myself to some extent from the more commercial performers to explore the politicals like Pete Seeger, Bluegrass, the blues (a love I shared with Stuart Lasine), and exotica such as Miriam Makeba or Marais and Miranda from South Africa. I guess classical performances were also something that continued to bind me to family, at least to my mother and her people. I still remember my first evening at the opera to see *The Flying Dutchman.* I remember hearing Casals and Stravinsky playing with the symphony orchestra. I remember sharing my parents' delight when we bought the LPs for Brecht and Weill's *Die Dreigroschenoper* (The Threepenny Opera). This sensibility, oozing cynicism and radical politics, was a natural for me.

As for my more romantic side, here is a poem I wrote, already fantasising about Africa, in the spring of 1962 and published in the school literary magazine.

To African Violets Blooming in April

The city is slowly warming,
Wiped clean of winter by gales of wind;
Not yet warmed by balmy sun rays,
Brown and bare and tender-skinned.

Yet in this bleak and dismal clime,
Shielded from winds by a windowpane,
Grow the beings exotic and sultry,
Nurtured by a gardener's rain.

Far from their native Africa,
Giving hope to me, impatient for May,
The violets sit on the windowsill
Bidding winter to be on its way.

At our fiftieth class reunion in 2012, there was no question who the star teacher was in the memories of most of us. This was Jim Inskeep, who had not had the opportunity to do a PhD at the University of Chicago but was a brilliant teacher who brought us a college-level textbook that covered world history in a comprehensive way, with major sections on Japan, China, India, and the Middle East as well as Europe. I really loved his classes and did extremely well, always getting the top mark and gaining self-confidence as a result. Jim was a very different character, politically libertarian, quite Scots, attracted to judo and Zen Buddhism. He was so unlike my social environment until then, yet I continued to find this fascinating and attractive. We had a few other capable teachers but Jim Inskeep was the real article. He once gave me as a present the liberal triumphalist W.W. Rostow's *Stages of Economic Growth*. Jim was no radical. However, the questions I ask today may represent a wavelength that I can trace right back to him.

I think as a teenager I was already acquiring many of the traits of an intellectual within what was a rather congenial and protected environment. But I hadn't much of an idea of the wider world and how I would fit into it. I had ideas about who I was that made sense in terms of my obsessive reading, my interest in history and public affairs, but very little in terms of my modest background as regards income and money: naive upper-middle-class ambitions based on working-class money! I can understand now how unlikeable this was to my father as a combination. The very close bond with my mother was also weakening. And neither parent provided me with a viable model of masculinity.

My cousins were both academic achievers too and they would both shift to the Ivy League in time, Jim as a Princeton undergraduate and Richard as a Columbia law student. I had the same idea in my head, but it was not to be. It was a turning point in my life and a yellow warning light that, when I applied for college entrance, I wound up with only one acceptance letter from my back-up school, the University of Chicago. At first I was shattered, depressed by this unexpected defeat. There was to be no great leap into some mystified but really unknown establishment world of my dreams and callow ambitions. If I think about why, I have to say that the interview processes must have marked me as naive, effeminate and somewhat preposterous, with a grand sense of entitlement belied by my lack of any accomplishment outside the classroom, least of all the kind of accomplishment that was expected of an American boy on the high road to success, one that would require a big scholarship. It is worth mentioning that other children I knew from this émigré milieu were generally eager to assimilate into North Side Chicago Jewish life and did not hold the same fascination that I did with the lost world of central Europe. I may have let loose with left-wing ideas that, to me, were just common sense, and my assumption that ideas and books were far and away what was important in life was neither universally held nor backed by any sense of reality. My comfortable highschool environment, matched by very good grades but not without weaknesses – notably in science – and extremely high scores on the supposedly objective testing mechanisms, was not going to be a prelude to easy future success. At university I would be successful enough as a history major to virtually forget about this startling end to my highschool years, but later it would come back to haunt me.

6 | As a Student: Chicago and Yale

My mother's family originally lived in Hyde Park when they first came from Vienna to Chicago and so did quite a few others from central Europe. In 1962 I returned here in a new capacity to start a very different kind of life as a University of Chicago undergraduate. Hyde Park was such a distinctive neighbourhood that it needs some attention to describe.

In the 1940s two major changes transformed this setting. Robert Hutchins, president of the university, became convinced, notably by Mortimer Adler, whose edition of what he considered the ultimate Western classics – 'the Great Books' – was then available, that US undergraduate education was superficial and pandered to the pleasures of an intellectually mediocre middle class. As a result, he introduced a curriculum that consisted exclusively of the 'Great Books'. You took an entrance exam to get in, regardless of whether you had a high school diploma or not, and when you finished the Great Books repertoire of courses – very demanding – you got a degree. From being in large part a university to which students either commuted or where they lived in fraternity or sorority houses, it became the site of a network of student apartments in which the university interfered not at all in the lives of their residents. This was a genuinely liberal environment and as a result it attracted students from academic and from left-wing families, including underground Communists. A symbolic Hutchins gesture was the dissolution of intercollegiate football, so rife with the symbolism of college as a middle-class resort of pleasure for male youth. Hutchins famously said that when the need for exercise arose in him, he would take a nap until the urge disappeared. One result is that enrolments fell drastically. However, there was generous scholarship money available for a large part of the undergraduates, and the professional schools such as Law and Medicine held their reputation as outstanding in the Middle West. Only a third of the students in my time were in fact undergraduates.

At the same time, the city of Chicago was also changing. Wartime brought many black families north up the Mississippi Valley and it was no longer possible to house them, even in crowded and overpriced apartments, on the South Side 'Black Belt'. As blacks tried to move out, a tense atmosphere flared up again when whites panicked and there were fears of major violence breaking out. As a result, the system changed: the real estate business began to redline specific blocks, in order to make space for black expansion, on the South and West Sides and the city's Democratic Party began to concede more clout and more space to its 'Negro' wing. By 1962, Hyde Park was turning into a white enclave in an otherwise black, segregated Near South Side. There was serious talk of moving the university to distant Colorado. Instead, the city became the site of a relatively sophisticated experiment decided ironically between the political party my parents voted for and my parents' two employers, the University of Chicago and Marshall Field's department store, anxious to keep downtown going as an active shopping precinct.[1] In effect, the university bought a lot of property and used its influence to police the Hyde Park neighbourhood and keep its white 'character'. There were worries that, between them, the Hutchins system and the blacks had led to a desertion of the university, particularly of its undergraduate core, by the affluent of Chicago. We had very few students coming from the array of wealthy North Shore or desirable western suburbs.

One answer to shrinkage and the anticipation of slender endowments in the future was to normalise the curriculum. By my time the Great Books were dominant in what we called General Education courses, but these made up only half your curriculum. Eventually you declared a major and moved on in the normal manner after four years. The university began to do what it could to recruit what it saw as normal young people rather than those who were attracted to an alternative lifestyle and an alternative politics. This process was getting under way in my day, but it clashed with the emergence nationally of the so-called Counter-Culture, fuelled by the civil rights movement and the growing hostility of the youth to America's foolish adventure in Vietnam.

I quickly took to this unusual environment and made it perhaps all too much my home. I remember, as I looked out of the window of my dormitory room and watched my parents drive away, feeling exuberant that this was basically the end of our joint lives. Their lives would make far more sense without this strange American child, and mine without these émigrés stuck between the values of the old country and the immigrant world they had entered. However, many of their values remained imprinted in me, sometimes in contradictory fashion, and probably also, at greater depth, their moods and temperaments.

Normally I took the Sheridan Road bus to the university. At Michigan and Randolph downtown, I descended to the Illinois Central station, bought a train ticket and sped off with only a distant glimpse of the South Side as the train whizzed down. For me a childish metaphor kept recurring: as in that children's classic film *The Wizard of Oz*, I left the world I knew (from which I was already somewhat alienated) – Kansas during the Great Depression, in black and white. When I got out in magical Hyde Park, the world took on colour just like the land of Oz. In my fantasy, this was a world of books and ideas where I could feel at home. What could be better than an evening in a library full of unknown wonders?

What was this oddball world like, with its declining student numbers (my class consisted at first of only about six hundred eighteen-year-olds, and there was a high drop-out rate), that was desperate enough to include me? The university retained its prestige as a postgraduate institution, notably for law and medicine. It had an impressive library and it was well funded, enough to keep the likes of me with good grades going on scholarships plus a bit extra from part-time university employment. Here are some of the things I remember. Forty per cent of the students were Jewish, the majority from Chicago or the cities of the East Coast; the sophistication of the New Yorkers was a striking tonic. The majority of the students, indeed even a quarter of the girls, were science majors. In the 1964 national election, the straw poll for the university gave Barry Goldwater, the Republican far-right libertarian, far under ten per cent of the total; they were mostly a small coterie of intellectual libertarians. Many students were the children of significant cultural figures and academics: authors Saul Bellow and William Saroyan, sociologists Daniel Bell and David Riesman, the conductor Erich Leinsdorf, Moses Asch of

Folkways Records, historian Jack Hexter, filmmaker Haskell Wexler, a Schocken from the once-European publishing house, and a Piore from the family with several star intellectuals, to name a few that I remember. And quite a few were so-called red diaper babies, sometimes with ersatz names which the parents had taken to avoid the McCarthy years' persecution of Communists. If you examine the alumni magazine over the years, you will find for my period very few conventional success stories, especially in the business world apart from a few start-ups and high techies. There are plenty of academics, plenty of workers in the NGO world, intellectuals of all sorts, as well as many who dropped out and never graduated. I remember guessing that maybe one per cent or somewhat less were sufficiently disturbed to be candidates for youth suicide. By this token, I started to feel like a regular guy, paying the rent and handing in my assignments invariably on time. I did brilliantly in history with straight As and I quickly came to feel confident that making a living as an historian would come naturally to me. Of course, there are other factors that make for a successful career, but of this I understood just about nothing.

To do well, you had to read a lot and study hard, but surrounding you was an American version of *la vie bohème*: after first year, most students lived in large shared apartments, and apartment Saturday night parties were legendary. Chicago students later described this university as a place 'where the fun dies'. This was perhaps true of fun as conceived in a Broadway musical or a wholesome movie set on a college campus, but if you wanted to open yourself up to a very different kind of world, the University of Chicago and Hyde Park were the place. There was booze and drugs. I thoroughly enjoyed my hallucinations in a couple of acid trips and had great times high on marijuana. Beyond this, I should mention the Documentary Films group (I volunteered as an usher), which exposed me to many of the great classics from Europe and America; the growing presence of rock and roll with the Paul Butterfield Blues Band as our reputed generic local; and the existence of experimental contemporary classical music and art. I remember puzzling my way through a Claes Oldenburg happening. I acted in twentieth-century classic plays. The burning issues of the day were discussed by Hans Morgenthau and Hannah Arendt in packed auditoriums. And we thought all the time about New York, about California, about Europe. For me this was a wonderful atmosphere compared with the post-war American scene in which I had grown up; one where I could grow and breathe.[2]

Interestingly, Arendt tended to defend the US role in Vietnam, in part due to her husband's intense anti-Communism as well as her admiration for an abstracted notion of US constitutionalism. But I also heard her debate with a conventional Jewish establishment spokesperson, Marie Syrkin, about the Eichmann trial and say, what were for some, unpardonable things about Jews who had chosen not to resist under the Nazi heel. She was not always correct in her historical sense (she tended to generalise too much from her own experience in France during the first months of Vichy) but her philosophical sense was very powerful. I liked very much her Germanness with the baritone voice and the never-ending cigarettes. There were numerous Europeans and others teaching at this liberal American university who created a homelier atmosphere for me. I also learnt from the debate how unpleasant establishment Jews could be.

My first history teacher and favourite was Emile Karafiol, a Polish-born Jew who had grown up in Canada but still had a faint Polish accent. He started us out with the French Revolution and the great left interpretations of Lefebvre and Soboul. As a general source, he gave us what was then a new text – Eric Hobsbawm's *The Age of Revolution, 1789 to 1848.* What was a marvel for me was Hobsbawm's erudition as well as his independent Marxism,[3] his seemingly effortless ability to explore philosophy, the arts, politics and economic change, and consider their interrelationships. He has remained for all these years my ultimate model of what an historian can hope to achieve. I did a great independent study with Karafiol of Weimar culture, systematically reading what were the exciting new ideas of my parents' youth.[4]

If I think about other teachers that I admired, I would have to say that they were a real grab bag covering very different areas. Anne Pippin Burnett explained how Greek tragedy had roots in a very unmodern and un-Western culture. A.K. Ramanujan, the great Tamil poet, read his own translations of thousand-year-old classics. Charles Gray, the charming husband of future university president Hanna Holborn Gray, gave a lovely course on seventeenth-century English intellectual life, and a Dutch émigré, Jock Weintraub, explained what he considered to be the mainly German tradition of *Geistesgeschichte*, or history of ideas.[5] This included

Perry Miller's famous study of the New England mind, which made a deep impression on me by helping me to understand where the US mentality came from. Arcadius Kahan, himself a veteran of the Polish Bund, the Jewish socialist party, organised a course on Jewish political life before the Holocaust in eastern Europe, for two of us. He was also an accomplished economic historian of Russia.

Thanks to the rave accounts of my friend Peter Weil, I shifted for English composition to a section led by Ronald Wiener. One day, as the rain poured down, we sat at the top of Cobb Hall, a building from the 1890s, and listened as Wiener read to us the first words of James Farrell's *Studs Lonigan*, a memorable novel about youth in working-class Irish Chicago in the inter-war years. And he pointed out that it was also in Cobb Hall in the afternoon as the rain poured down that Farrell got the idea of writing this novel, which made him famous. This was a far cry from Lake View High School, and yet to a considerable extent Farrell reverberated with the Chicago in which I had grown up.

I regretted the absence of economics from these ideas. Our then eccentric economics star, Milton Friedman, ran a department which required calculus for the basic course to discourage the amateurs and which was typically and deeply unintegrated into the study of history more generally. In our comprehensive course, John Stuart Mill was the most modern economist we were set to read, with the exception of John S. Knight, a one-time laissez-faire eminence at the university. I was the one who hauled out the reserve books for the graduate students in the Business and Economics Library, and I observed this arcane and notoriously reactionary subject matter from a distance. Friedman was still considered very idiosyncratic if brilliant; his time hadn't come.

I took no US history at all. The truth is that most US history in this era, especially of the twentieth century, was tedious and lacking in ideas as well as disconnected from the rest of the world. This would change as people of my generation pushed at the door with new thoughts, new heroes and an eagerness to rescue so much that was left out from the conventional stuff. I did very much enjoy work like C. Wright Mills's *The Power Elite* (1965), which explained the US to me as a real society from my sheltered vantage point.

It is difficult to explain now why I decided to try to put together a major in African history (there was no real historian of Africa present yet) and why I didn't proceed with European history, where my skills obviously lay. Given my poor understanding of the profession and my lack of contact with real live historians, I felt – naively – that European history was probably overpopulated with scholars concerned with the finer details, while Africa seemed wide open. My first explorations suggested that the Africana works in the library were rarely historical in character but rather dominated by current events books and anthropology, which largely repelled me. What about an African history that focused on the twentieth century, with colonialism, nationalism and so on as the centrepieces of study? I like to think I approached the subject without a racial lesson to learn. Black people evoked curiosity but not a desire to crusade on their behalf. Colonialism was obviously a complicated subject. I wasn't attracted to writing about the slave trade. The one person who made an impression on me and who handled Africa really interestingly was the political scientist Aristide Zolberg (of course, another European). Zolberg was fascinating when he talked about politics in the Ivory Coast and compared it to the boss system in Chicago, which I knew well. He was less interesting when immersing us in US modernisation or development theory, much of which seemed simplistic and formulaic to me. I did well in the exam nonetheless, but it made me feel I was getting away with something and I resolved to avoid political science in future.

Our courses were demanding, with relatively low grades for lots of study. It was important to me later as a teacher to have had to explore all the classics first-hand, a lot of Freud, Durkheim and Weber, of Adam Smith, Thomas Malthus, David Ricardo and John Stuart Mill, of Thucydides, Aristotle (a Chicago favourite) and Plato, of Galileo and Darwin.[6] I also acquired at least a primitive sense of how to talk about art, architecture and music as well as literature. In the required social science sequence, we all had to read some of the newly available Karl Marx discussions of alienation from the *Grundrisse* and other sources that preceded his discovery of Engels and the Industrial Revolution. I have to pay tribute to my section teacher, Dick Flacks, who helped explain sympathetically this initially very difficult Hegelian language and connect it to reality. Dick never got tenure at Chicago although it was an historian of the new school, Jesse Lemisch, on whose behalf there was considerable protest when he was denied a position. This brings me to some of the things that I liked less about Chicago and gradually came to understand better.

One day walking down the road I passed by a couple of black girls and excused myself as I went by. One said to the other that this was the first time a white person had ever excused himself for anything in her presence. I thought this was quite rude but was also very embarrassed. I became gradually aware of our spatial context, of this middle-class island separated from the ghetto, and it seemed wrong to me even if it made possible the delightful intellectual environment of Hyde Park.

I also remember finding, later on in my undergraduate years, a volume that went through the university's history in the McCarthy era and the consequent purges that affected the University of Chicago, as they did virtually all US institutions. I finally became aware that, at least from 1965, people who saw the world politically, as I was doing more clearly – identifying with socialism and being hostile to the Cold War – were generally unwelcome in US academic life, even in genuinely liberal environments. Of course, this very orientation was critical in keeping this island of liberty functioning despite its many non-establishment features. Both these signal moments started to free me to understand my context better, but I have to say that I was still fundamentally naive and fundamentally complacent about my life when I graduated from college in 1966. For me the expanding range of interests, of intellectual and cultural adventures that marked these years, were hopefully just the beginning of a US that would change radically. Jack Kennedy's assassination, a startling event in 1963, marked perhaps a turning point in the comfortable conformity of the previous decade, an entrée into real history.

This may be a good place to say something about the political ambience of the time. The University of Chicago was at the forefront of a youth movement that was deservedly known as the Counter-Culture. Out of this counter-cultural soil, a range of important shoots sprang up: black nationalism, the feminist movement, the green movement, the gay movement. I saw the point of all these, but none of them really spoke to my personal enthusiasms or interests. My prejudices, my background and my intellectual interests put the emphasis rather on the Cold War and Vietnam.

I was fascinated to read in the works of authors such as William Appleman Williams or I.F. Stone that the post-war Soviet Union was essentially defensive in outlook and would have preferred a neutral Germany on the lines of Austria. Cold-blooded US action to defend reactionaries in Iran or Guatemala had struck me for years as outrageous, and in Vietnam it seemed to me that the US had set itself up as the champion of reaction once the French were beaten. I not only opposed the war and had no intention of signing up for conscription, but I actively hoped the US would be taught a lesson in Vietnam that would end its overbearing conviction that it had a right to run the world. Policies such as the restoration of the Shah and the non-recognition of China seemed idiotic. As I read more about black politics in the US, I saw the point of separatist politics, but this also seemed to me both unpleasant and a cul-de-sac. Integration in the context of major social reform and an abolition of the ghetto was the way to go. There was no black separatism that I knew about in Cuba, and the Cuban Revolution, with its ideals and its goal of changing entirely what Cuba was assumed to stand for in the world, I admired fiercely and had already done so for some years. My tolerance of black separatism would increase later when I began to know black people better.

On the whole, I admired those with the guts to stand up and say their mind, just as I felt about those who actually went south and at real risk promoted the civil rights cause.[7] In my final year as an undergraduate, we occupied the Administration Building and held a very big anti-war sit-in. I found this exhilarating, liberating from the perspective of the temporary disappearance of normality, normal days, normal authority patterns, normal habits. But I was only a foot soldier and played no role of any significance. I became ever more conversant with US and other left literature and culture but, while I thought much of what they said was spot on, I was not attracted to sign up with any of the small Marxist sects that existed, barely, on our campus. The other side of the coin was that I was struck by how outraged many faculty members were at what seemed to them beyond the respectable and the norm. Their level of tolerance was surprisingly narrow. I also had my first good view of national media and was startled to learn that the news was contested and that objective reporting was not necessarily what the establishment press offered.

I have not said much about my friends in college. This was, indeed, a very different and sometimes lonely period of life compared to high school. Apart from Peter Weil, the son of German émigré parents, who made me feel comfortable and whom I had known from primary school, my memories are that I explored with varying enthusiasm different people with different talents and, after a time, I moved on.

I should mention my final-year fellow tenants on 5108 S. Kimbark (round the corner from the future Obama household). Ray Schrag was the son of well-off German émigrés, too, who had a lovely sprawling home in suburban New York. Ray's parents established themselves in Belgium in the 1930s and then, in good time, moved on to the US. His lawyer-father collected autographs of eminent authors, his one uncle was the German translator of Hemingway who had returned to the family business in Karlsruhe and the other a successful landscape artist who had come under the influence of Marsden Hartley and his wonderful pictures of forest and sea in Maine. The Schrags were an interesting combination of European and American, they were very nice to me, and Ray, a keen rock climber, was definitely a much-admired role model whose overt masculinity occasionally embarrassed but also attracted me. The Schrags also provided a kind of model of how to balance Europe and America that was different from the uncomfortable accommodation I knew from home. The second roommate, Michael Lieber, was the son of a pair of Polish socialists who managed to steal a horse in Drohobycz, the oil capital of Nazi-occupied Galicia, and flee behind Russian lines, thus surviving right in the wake of the Holocaust. Michael himself was born in Krakow after the war ended. He would follow me to Yale, and became an anthropologist and later a filmmaker. The third boy, Paul Mittelman, was a lovely individual from Queens, eager to stand out as a good student, as a newly minted radical, a somewhat undersized football player and motorbike enthusiast. He died in 1969 in suspicious circumstances, killed in a supposed accident by a policeman in Maine when involved in some summer-term legal aid activity.

Another friend who deserves some attention was Tom Leighton. He was, and is, a unique character. We became fast friends right from the start of the orientation period; we had rooms fairly close to each other and he was a regular part of my life for the remainder of my Chicago time as well as for decades after. Tom went to an elite Catholic school in a Boston suburb; he had a mixed Irish–WASP background, less rare than it may seem in New England. He was very tall and very thin with some handsome dark Irish looks. Tom was bright but lazy and he shared my fascination with other cultures. Astonishingly, his school taught him a more than passable French – he truly loved France – and he had sophisticated and often astringent tastes in classical music, art and literature, not to speak of his growing knowledge of food and wine. He majored in Arabic studies and was a student of Marshall Hodgson, a figure who belied the Saidian template of Eurocentrism in his famous explorations of medieval Arab mysticism and classicism and who, if anything, has grown in stature since his death. Despite Tom's indifferent grades, he could have carried on with this as a postgrad but didn't. When I met Tom, he was recovering from Catholicism and beginning to explore his homosexuality. I imagine he found me, effeminate little wimp that I was, a fellow explorer potentially, but in fact he put up with me despite disappointment in this sphere. Tom himself did not find a suitable partner for many years and I became a kind of acolyte in his cultural enrichment programme. He was overbearing and occasionally arrogant; I would get tired of the endless pressure to fit into his odd nocturnal schedule, but he needed a partner to share adventures and, in short to medium doses, he was a generous friend from whom I learnt an enormous amount. He was also perhaps the first close friend I made from an utterly different background from my own.

It is not surprising what I got as a graduation present: a trip to the much-dreamt-of Old World – a summer in Europe. I can remember the itinerary well: first England, then a flight to Paris on my twenty-second birthday, then the train to Munich for a few days and on to Salzburg, and then Vienna for a week. From Vienna I survived the hard wooden seats of the two-night train trip through the Balkans to Athens. In Athens I signed up for a tour of the best-known mainland sights and a few days on the then pretty unspoilt Aegean island of Ios.

The return trip started with the ferry to Brindisi and then on by train to Florence. From Milan I flew back to London to catch the flight home. There was nothing I didn't enjoy. I saw the art and architecture for real and not in pictures. I spoke French comprehensibly and found a whole country where people spoke Austrian German. The light and the sea in Greece gave it a special magic. There were a few interesting encounters. I remember

Figure 6.1: Riding a donkey on Ios, Greece, 1966

chatting on the train through Italy with a very liberal American priest who was the right-hand man in St Louis of the last pre-war Austrian chancellor, Kurt Schuschnigg. I remember Greek couples dancing on the table aboard the ferry through the night as we sailed from Athens to Ios, Zorba the Greek come to life. Young Europeans offered me places to stay, and there were many friendly exchanges in every country. I didn't quite recover from Americanitis – the inability to manage without the familiar and the banal – but it was a condition that steadily weakened. I felt in Europe I had a persona that was much closer to the average than in America, and the lifelong sense of having to be watchful about coming into contact with non-intellectuals, people who would understand nothing in common with me, faded too.

I also had encounters with various family friends and relatives, often adding a new perspective to what I had known since boyhood. The family stories became far more real. In England, where the largest single number of Austrian Jewish refugees had settled, there was my mother's best friend, an unmarried teacher of retarded children, and her mother.

There was my grandmother's Hungarian cousin Zsofia, who had finally left her native country in the wake of the 1956 Revolution; there was her brother, the economist Djurka Katona, and his wife and daughter, all with Hungarian charm and vitality; and there was Marianne, my mother's very intelligent and politically alive younger second cousin, who had spent the summers of her youth with my mother and aunt, also a teacher of children with special needs, in Bristol. With Marianne it was possible to talk about politics and cultural and social issues; she had been forced out of the University of Vienna in 1938 after her first year.

Within the family, I could see a political spectrum. The Hungarians were certainly liberals and Djurka's daughter Agi worked for Radio Free Europe. Another Hungarian cousin by way of Australia and living in Paris was Peter Lengyel, who founded the *Journal of Social Science* for UNESCO but whose memoir shows his frustration as a liberal at the rise of Third World nationalism.[8] On the other hand, aunt Fritzi's niece Liesl, one of her few surviving relatives, was a senior official in the foreign ministry of Communist Hungary.

Figure 6.2: With my mother's friends Lenchen and Georgiana Dukes in the garden of their home in Sutton, London, 1966

Finally there was an eye-popping visit to my uncle's brother Ernest, as he now was, and his family. Ernest had become a Cambridge don replete with pipe and a love of puns (which he shared with my Winnetka uncle, his brother) and crossword puzzles (at which he was far better than I was). He had become a perfect Conservative-voting English gentleman who often spent holidays in a houseboat on the Broads. The suburban-style Frankl house looked a bit like the familiar house in Winnetka, but off we drove to visit his two brothers-in-law, the literary critic Graham Hough and Tom Clucas, the man who before 1938 represented the Frankl family business in England, one in a Tudor cottage and the other in a Jacobean country house. Here was a dimension of life that fitted to a T my ambitions and tastes, of which I had known very little. I hit it off with Clare, the younger child and then a schoolgirl. Clare's moment of fame was to come years later when, fairly fresh out of Cambridge, she was put forward as a feminist candidate for the headship of the Royal Academy of Architects. This is a friendship that continued through the years, and she is probably the family member, admittedly not a blood relation, with whom I feel the greatest affinity.

Vienna itself was perhaps the one disappointment. The summer of 1966 was a very wet, cool one and this did not show off to advantage the heavy-set stone architecture of imperial Vienna, lugubrious compared with Paris. Moreover, the archetype set by Hugo Bettauer in the inter-war classic *Stadt ohne Juden* (City without Jews) had come true. The Jews were virtually gone and the people you saw in the street, even in the centre, looked like hicks, the women with feather-bedecked hats and the men in loden jackets and lederhosen.[9] In the novel, of course, the Jews came back. In 1960s Vienna only a few came back and the city had been losing population for half a century. And here I had almost no contacts with family members. I did have a nice evening on the Kahlenberg with my grandmother's slightly flamboyant best friend from her youth, Ella Erdös, who had returned from exile in Britain after she lost her husband and son. Ella missed the Vienna of her past very much, and once the 1955 treaty was signed guaranteeing Austrian neutrality, she returned. She gave me a sense of what the family milieu had once been like *in situ*.

I understood this voyage in the sense of what it promised in future life. Here finally I connected to the real thing. Given my high grades, the University of Chicago History Department gave me the support I needed, with no feeling of trouble ahead. On this basis, I got a scholarship to Yale, which was considered a very desirable department of history for a graduate student and prospective academic. I thought, as my father put it, that I now had it made. This seemed to make up for the defeat of 1962 and I was delighted at the idea of moving to the East Coast, only a two-hour bus or train trip from Manhattan. So I started the new academic year feeling in a good place and full of confidence about what lay ahead. My new and more intellectually connected sense of family, my excitement about the youth revolution as it seemed in America, my self-confidence as a student of history, all came together.

My sensibility in the Yale years can perhaps be gauged from this poem I wrote. I was thinking of a friend from high school, Jane Goldberg (later Diao, 1945–2017), who went into the Peace Corps right after college in 1966.

To Jane in Fatick

I look out at a baobab,
I don't work very hard,
A Peace Corps girl in the Senegal
Trying to forget Bernard.
I work in the Social Center,
And teach the Wolof ladies to sew,
I walk among the groundnut fields
And watch the brown Sine flow.
Six thousand miles away, I grew up
In a gray glass city on a lake.
When I go back there, I don't know now
I might crack there, I might break.
But I've been swallowed in Africa,
Alone with my language and my self,
The mosquito nets on the bedding,
And the English books on the shelf.

On the riverbank there lives a carpenter
Every morning he says – you can guess,
And some night when the African moon

87

Rises high and yellow –
I might
Say
Yes.

I certainly never felt at home in New Haven. Here, too, I can give an envisioned metaphor, this time one from a recurring nightmare. It was forever summer, a humid but airless summer in which one was trapped and pent up between East and West Rocks. Time had to be devoted to sitting on the floor in some academic building waiting, waiting for the professor to make a brief appearance during his infrequent 'office hours'. I was unable really to live anywhere. I moved around furnished digs and felt uncertain about where my books and other few possessions were located. This recurrent dream presented New Haven as a form of prison.

The next two years, 1966–1968, were by no means unhappy and the nightmares began considerably later. The extraordinary wealth of Sterling Library (with an excellent Africanist specialist in the Ulsterman Moore Crossey) was an ocean of knowledge. I did enjoy living in a small city dating back to the seventeenth century. I met some very interesting people as well and, as we shall see shortly, the intermediate summer break in California was delightful. But Yale as an institution was something else. I quickly learnt that we graduate students were in a way the hired help; the place was about its undergraduates, if not its faculty, and these were highly respectable and well placed in US society. They included Bill Clinton and George W. Bush. The typical Yale undergraduate aimed at reasonable, not outstanding, marks, lived in the East, and was headed for Wall Street or at least some sort of moneyed business career. This was still a college exclusively for men. There were Jewish professors and students, certainly, but this was still predominantly a WASP institution and, to some extent, a foreign land for me.

In these first years, life seemed good and I can recount a number of positive things that filled these days apart from Sterling Memorial Library. Almost as large as the library was the temple-like gym. Here I could work out, running (rather pathetically slowly) and, more satisfactorily, building up muscles at last. This I enjoyed very much. Interestingly, beyond the gym lay a New Haven which was afflicted in that direction with the same problems as the South Side of Chicago: the encroaching ghetto – but it wasn't often a direction that I took. Yale with New Haven has in recent decades had to deal with the problems of a decaying city with serious social ills.

There was no equivalent at Yale of the Chicago immersion in the Great Books. History especially lacked any orientation to common purpose or common theoretical vision. At most I can acknowledge the role of William Roger Louis, now of the University of Texas, when taking a class on imperialism through copies of official nineteenth-century British correspondence, in helping to allow me to move from being a voracious reader of history to becoming a potential historian able to work with classic archival sources. It is hard for me to think what I learnt from the junior Africanist at Yale, Maynard Swanson. This is ironic in so far as Swanson wrote about my future home city, Durban, and is rightly considered a pioneer in writing about South African urban history. But he taught nothing of this, and all his writing occurred well after he was bumped from Yale, an untenured faculty member. I can remember him informing me that Yale had the huge hurdle of a double language requirement. He clearly did not know what to say when I responded that I was sure I could pass the required tests in German and in French. We really did not connect as human beings at all. In fact, I might mention here that I had an excellent language teacher named Mrs Broekhuizen, who did some of the language preparation teaching for the department but who had enough customers to offer a course in her native Dutch, which I can say I learnt properly – *een vlotte Nederlands* – its remarkable pronunciation included. In addition, I used some spare hours in New Haven to teach myself basic Italian; that was just for pleasure. Swanson's departure was followed by the arrival in 1969 of Leonard Thompson, a liberal South African, who could be considered a moderate opponent of apartheid. Leonard was a fluent writer but there was little in his ideas or approach that interested me.

Unsurprisingly, it was two European émigré professors who did impress me. One was the fearsome medievalist, Robert(o) Lopez, historian of Genoa. I found his approach to medieval history, based on commerce and political interest rather than the church, fascinating. He had a brilliant mind, but I cannot forget watching him humiliate at least one American fellow student. Lopez was an Italian Jew, clearly on his way to the academic top when Mussolini's turn to anti-Semitism took him out of his own country. I encountered Lopez because of the good requirement that we do a field in pre-modern history (perhaps today one could substitute one from outside the West).

The other émigré was Heinz or Jindrich (later Harry) Benda from Moravská Ostrava in my ancestral country of Czechoslovakia. Fate took him, as a young man in the employ of the originally Czech firm of Bata, to the Dutch East Indies and, as a result, unlike his whole family, he survived the war. Benda was one of the first writers in America on South East Asia and I wanted to learn more about Vietnam. I was fortunate to be easily accepted socially by the little crowd of specialist students attracted to Benda – but his specialty was Indonesia. During the war years, he was a prisoner of the Japanese, but they did not single him out in any way as a Jew, which impressed him. And by chance he became very close to a fellow prisoner, a Dutch teacher who was fascinated with the political ferment of these years. Wim Wertheim, already very critical of Dutch colonialism, was moving towards the Marxism and Maoism that he pursued in post-war years as a scholar in Holland.[10] Harry became fascinated too and wrote a major assessment of the period of Japanese occupation in Indonesia (when the future president Sukarno chose to collaborate, to accept independence from the Japanese, and eventually to fight the returning Netherlanders). What he offered was not only an appreciation of the pre-colonial kingdoms of South East Asia and the civilisations behind them, but a structural sense of colonialism and nationalism of a kind I could not easily trace among the Africanists. This was a template of sorts for me. He also had a sense of the problems of development and a sympathy for radical alternatives to the conventional Western nostrums. His distaste for the US in Vietnam was such that he was in negotiations to move to Australia when he sadly died at an early age of a heart attack.

The final faculty member I should mention was an American whose well-reputed class I attended: Robert S. Thompson, the expert on Yoruba art. Thompson was somewhat flamboyant and certainly enthusiastic. However, his basic message, that you have to understand African pre-colonial art in terms of African culture in the way it was to be viewed, why it had been made, and how Africans understood this craft, was also eye-opening. I learnt to admire these art forms, mainly sculpture, quite separately from where they fitted into modernist European reworkings à la Braque or Picasso.

I guess my social life was slightly more interesting at Yale than it had been in Chicago. But the nature of the research project meant that people came and went. Good friendships made a real impact but did not last. I could mention two men who were later to be very successful in publishing, Doug Gibson and Frank Kauffman. Doug was a genuine Scotsman, probably my first good friend from outside the US, and I have learnt that he has made a great impact in promoting serious Canadian literature in Toronto, where he has spent his life. Frank was the son of a New Yorker wealthy enough to devote his time to his collection of books on Napoleon rather than working and his ex-wife was a charming woman whose parents were wealthy Cubans and whose friends included the wonderful and much-loved (by me) cartoonists and reviewers from the *New Yorker*, Charles Addams and company. Frank was a potential Russianist, but he found the heavy hand of the anti-Communist discourse oppressive and he ended up as a Manhattan lawyer for the publishing industry. And with Frank, I would often hang around with Peter Bradley, an artist who claimed to be the son of the jazz musician Miles Davis. I don't know if this was true, but Peter had the athleticism, the nerve, the wit and the charm of so many black Americans. If he didn't gobble up good-looking women, you wouldn't guess it from his conversation. And he was definitely the protégé of the mobile creator Alexander Calder. He had real Calders in his room. I could go on about people I met during these years, but this would only be to drop names and bring back the past for a moment as pure sentiment.

However, I do need to recall with great pleasure the summer of 1967 when I was offered money to go and study Swahili at the University of California (UCLA). After Chicago and Yale, UCLA was a wonderful never-never land where winter never came and fun was not at all a dirty word. Nor were the pretensions of Yale (which seemed to me rather like a starchy imitation of Oxbridge) present. The students in the class were mostly great fun and two years later I took advantage of the acquaintance to visit several who had fanned out and were busy doing research in East Africa. Our teacher was very good. I picked up, and retain to this day, a basic sense of the structure of Kiswahili, how to speak it correctly, comprehensibly and precisely, if very haltingly. Learning a non-European language is itself, as was Thompson's course on African art, a way of discovering different ways of self and group expression, different aesthetics and ways of looking at life.

We also had a wonderful teaching assistant, Noorjehan Zaidi, a lady from Mombasa, apparently the second woman from coastal Kenya ever to go to university (excluding, I suppose, Indians and Europeans). When she wasn't in Los Angeles (where she boarded with one of the showbiz Ritz Brothers), she was doing a degree at Sarah Lawrence College in New York. She was an endearing and vivacious language teacher who made the course come alive every day. Here was a Muslim woman who lived in an overwhelmingly black country (her personal background was Arabo-Indian), and she could not have been more three-dimensional and open.

When the course ended, I carried on for a fortnight to San Francisco. Here I stayed with and saw assorted friends from University of Chicago days while connecting, to the limited extent I could, with my father's family in the city. This was really the era of 'if you're going to San Francisco, be sure to wear some flowers in your hair', as the song went. The alternative culture which I had so liked in Chicago, which had very little presence in New Haven and not so much in Los Angeles, was now peaking on the peninsula. I stayed in Haight-Ashbury with a former University of Chicago roommate, Paul Soloff. In Berkeley I bought the rock concert posters I still treasure. I can remember a traffic jam crossing the Golden Gate Bridge, where joints were passed from car to car in this magnificent physical setting. It wasn't anymore the unspoilt beautiful countryside I had seen with my parents as a three-year-old, but it did seem a bit like heaven.

And if I think of family connections, I did meet men who, other than my Winnetka uncle, were principal figures in the social life my mother had known in Vienna. In particular, I spent time with Kurt Schwarz, the antiquarian bookseller. He and his wife had met in Shanghai where they spent the war years. Kurt used that time to become an expert in Chinese art and arrived in America with a trove of Chinese art books to sell. He had some formidable intellectuals in his own crowd of friends (the Islamicist Gustave von Grunebaum, Viennese of course, and the famous art critic Sir Ernst Gombrich, with whom my mother, not very happily, went out briefly around 1936) and his sympathies were left-wing when it came to Asia. He was far more appealing to me than any of the family crowd in Chicago, and I had a very good time visiting the Schwarz family in Brentwood.

If I think of my friends in New Haven, I have to mention a little group of Jewish men that I met on my return from my research year in Africa:

Charlie Friedman (who gave up the project and became a Chicago lawyer), Bob Schulzinger (the University of Colorado US diplomatic historian) and, above all, Fred Cooper. I arrived back in January 1970 and needed a place to stay; Fred's air stewardess girlfriend had just left him and he needed a tenant. Bob and the very amusing Charlie shared an apartment in the same building. This was incredible luck. Fred was not only a good friend but also a great intellectual partner. We traded ideas and thoughts constantly on our professors, our readings, the continent we were studying, and, I hope, learnt a lot from each other. Fred enjoyed and cooked great food; he loved classical music. As his father had worked for years for a Swiss drug company and his parents spent that time in Basel, Fred was very at ease in Europe and loved French ways. His open friendliness often belied a perspective on people and things that was as accurate as it was sharp. Today Fred is perhaps regarded as the top Africanist historian in the US although he writes more generally about empire and colonialism as well. By contrast to a Swanson or a Leonard Thompson, he offered arresting ideas with which to confront African facts as well as an ability to step out of his US shoes in cultural understanding. He is universally respected, and I cannot get over the good fortune I had in encountering him at this point in time.

7 | As a Student: Africa and England

Beginning in 1969, I had my first real encounter with Africa, itself part of a more complicated trajectory through Europe as well. This was a long and wonderful trip, lasting more than a year, which I was very sorry to bring to an end. To give a simple account, it can be divided into four parts. The first was a phase of three months which I spent researching for my PhD in the Dutch archives and living in The Hague. The second was a further archival research phase, this time in Cape Town. The third was a remarkable trip through Africa based on the way flights could be arranged and paid for in those days: to Lesotho, Kenya and Tanzania, Ethiopia, Egypt and out via Cyprus. The fourth was harder to justify. Reunited with my fieldnotes (index cards!) faithfully taken to Oxford by a South African DPhil student, Chris Saunders, aboard a Union-Castle liner, which still transported people from the Cape to Southampton, I spent the last months starting to write up my thesis as a visitor to St Antony's College, Oxford. But those few months had the biggest long-term consequences.

In Africa, I certainly had a stunning time encountering the antiquities of Egypt and Ethiopia, seeing some of the awesome scenery of East Africa (Ngorogoro Crater, Lake Naivasha, Kilimanjaro) and, following my introduction to Kiswahili in UCLA, having an enjoyable look at the East African coast where the classic coastal culture spoke to me. It was sufficiently urban and had enough charm and handicraft and cuisine to appeal to me. I should be dishonest if I did not admit that the more typical African village culture that I saw, often through the eyes of young American researchers and Peace Corps volunteers whom I visited, did not draw me in. Much of the historiography of Africa as it was then developing (under the strong influence of the University of Wisconsin) was virtually ethnographic, explorations of the minds of the typical villagers, sufficiently localised to make generalisations beyond a point very difficult. In effect African history was colonised by the better-developed field of anthropology. While I admired the best fieldwork expositions, I could not say that I was taken with the theoretical ideas in anthropology or its general project. I wanted to make a history for Africa that was historical and that could be placed alongside the histories of the other continents, and I wanted to focus on what I felt was the big picture while being sensitive to social nuance, incisive and not superficial.

South Africa in 1969 was in a phase of quietude and repression. The African National Congress (ANC), not to mention its rivals, was nowhere to be seen and the government seemed to have matters in hand. The alternative youth culture sweeping America and Europe did not exist; I remember thinking that after three months I could virtually recognise all of the half-dozen white males in the city of Cape Town who wore long hair. They were massively outnumbered by elderly chaps in khaki shorts and blazers who clearly wished to identify first and foremost with their World War II service. Most pop music that I liked, most films I had seen or intended to see, were banned. And yet South Africa, archaic as it was considered to be, seemed to be doing very well indeed economically despite a stock market blip. This was surprising.

Given my proclivities, much of what I had read about the politics of the country suggested crisis and acute tension. The most important writers on South Africa in America spent much of their time on the black opposition and its antecedents and prospects, often with a clear preference for more racial nationalist types than any prospective or real Communists.[1] Yet, in reality, this political arena was almost entirely invisible or closed off in 1969. I was also amazed and sometimes fascinated by the strange political contortions exhibited by moderate white liberals who clearly wanted their own class and culture, their own worlds, to be preserved but were looking for some kind of constitutionally acceptable situation that could also accommodate the black majority in a way that retained their unchallengeable ties to the West, especially big daddy Britain.

When I think back on this time, I remember two things that influenced me a lot. One was a weekend afternoon when I went to Muizenberg on the little southern suburbs train to sun myself at this beautiful False Bay beach.

There on the pier were a clutch of little old ladies speaking a language completely incomprehensible to me. But when I thought it through, I realised that these were Jewish women born in eastern Europe speaking to one another in Yiddish. And somehow the insight that hit me was that these individuals and their families had also given a great deal to South Africa and were crucial to its making. They had as much legitimacy to be South African as anyone else. Why was this different from the situation of equivalent women in the US? Ending apartheid, and the discrimination and exclusion that went with it, was one thing, but privileging the indigenes as though this were Ghana or Zambia didn't really appeal to me.

The second was a process, not an event. Partly for pleasure and partly for practical ends, I taught myself Afrikaans (which I still speak haltingly with a Dutch accent) and began to explore Afrikaans literature. Afrikaner folkways can seem stifling to an outsider, but I was very impressed at the quality and sophistication of the best stuff, much more impressive than anything in English. I also realised that writers such as Ingrid Jonker and Breyten Breytenbach were hardly tools of the regime. All this didn't make me a champion of a white exceptional case in South Africa but rather, despite it all, a champion for a future such as we would call integration in the US. And it aroused in me a curiosity as to what this fascinating mix of people were capable of producing. The ANC (and, even more so, its rivals, notably the Pan Africanist Congress breakaway), despite claims to 'non-racialism', was powered by a strong racial nationalist component that I found very unattractive and, indeed, still do. This didn't turn me into a fan of apartheid, but it made me unwilling to accept some idea of 'black liberation' as a goal that inspired me. I was certainly pleased with those on the left who imagined major reforms in labour, welfare and opportunities – a politics of class – and I suppose I have thought that the Cuban Revolution, which never stressed racial issues in isolation, was a good model for South Africa. Broadly speaking, this is still my basic perspective although it is sufficiently singular to make it seem pointless to advocate more than very occasionally. In England, I did begin to have indirect contact with the Unity Movement (largely Coloured, or mixed race, in membership), which has never been able to maintain a strong practical presence in South Africa but whose dominant ideas about culture and race are probably the only ones that have appealed to me. I was very impressed by Neville Alexander in particular when his key book, *One Azania, One Nation* (written under the pseudonym No Sizwe), came out in the 1970s and was heartily sorry that there wasn't a substantial national organisation behind it.

Without much thought, I had agreed with Maynard Swanson's suggestion that I write my PhD on the last phase of Dutch rule at the Cape, during the era of the Napoleon-inspired Batavian Republic. My only real idea here, beyond being interested in getting to know Holland, which sounded like a very attractive country, was that it might be interesting to explore the South African conundrum as a career by starting early – virtually the beginning of the nineteenth century. There are a number of further ideas that took hold of me during the course of this project, but I will confine myself here to two. The first was the importance of slavery; the largest number of Cape inhabitants in this period were enslaved and there was clearly a need to see this in terms of the colonial world of that time. The relationship of slave to slaveholder was the dominant driving force in the society. I would eventually find the Marxist idea of mode of production useful here.

What wasn't driving society was race, and that was my second idea. There were so many factual anomalies unthinkable in 1970 as regards the flexible boundaries of race that I slowly came to recognise that race did not have the importance or power for people in the Cape until sometime into the nineteenth century (and under British auspices). Race could be dealt with flexibly to fit circumstances, and the Dutch Cape conformed to the flexible norms of the eighteenth-century European colonies in Asia. Cape Town's world was really a maritime empire that stretched across the seas all the way to Japan. This was an important insight for me for understanding power in society and one that dreary Anglo-Saxon liberals mostly resisted, always convinced of their own reasonableness. Their view was to identify racism as an atavistic social element, strongest on the frontier, that came with the 'Dutchmen'. In fact, as Martin Legassick has shown, the racial frontiers were often very vague on the colonial frontier where different social elements interacted. There was plenty of racial prejudice but it was not true that society was actually structured around racial identity. Ever after, I have been interested in uncomfortable social facts and in people who fit in poorly as well as how they fared in the broad discourse of society.

I got to know Martin Legassick, who became an important friend, in London, where we both attended the legendary Southern African Studies seminars organised at the School of Oriental and African Studies (SOAS) by Shula Marks. One of the fortuitous meetings of importance in my life came about as a result of Shula's first sabbatical coinciding with my time in South Africa. As we ate anchovy toast over lunch in the Gardens in Cape Town, she asked if I wouldn't like to present a paper on my work to her seminar when I got to England. In fact, my paper was the first to be published in the first seminar series. I would not especially recommend it to readers now, but the seminar would prove to be a life-transforming experience. This was the seedbed of what came to be called revisionism. It led in various directions, but Martin in particular was an exciting and amazing change from the well-intended, somewhat paternalist liberalism of most English writing on South Africa. His papers from the 1970s dramatically changed my own outlook on South Africa. The history that was being explored notably by the sociologist Harold Wolpe, and then by somewhat younger historians such as Charles van Onselen, Peter Delius, Colin Bundy and William Beinart, looked far more closely at material, especially economic, factors while exploring what we now call social history. Another key participant was the Oxford historian Stan Trapido. There were many others, including activists, who would give a paper or pitch in from time to time at Shula's seminars.

This was a whole new wonderful world compared with what was offered by the Swansons and Thompsons. Martin, in fact, who had a family connection to Thompson, had done his PhD under him at UCLA, but he found the English environment more engaging. I too felt part of an exciting intellectual community that was building itself up by fits and starts. I was very fortunate to find myself in this nursery of new ideas with a sense of ferment and connectedness that contrasted drastically to Yale. At Yale everything revolved around one's relationship to a member of staff (and had I been more sophisticated, I would have realised this meant only a tenured member of staff like Thompson, not Swanson). Only when a visitor happened to come through did a seminar take place and it was just a decorative moment, not at all essential to the learning process.

Today it is necessary to say that the radical project was an overwhelmingly white one. These were the outstanding white intellectuals who wanted to get beyond and break with the paternalism of the liberal past. Some tried to speak in the name of blacks who had rebelled or taken an autonomous cultural path while others, more in my own vein, were concerned to create a structural mould that would explain key aspects of South Africa. This absence probably made the seminars less conflictual but also did reflect a real gap. In fact, the ANC was very well represented in London, where the exile movement had its headquarters, but the adherents who were active in the seminars were largely the 'non-blacks'. Harold Wolpe, as with some others, felt very free to speak his mind precisely, challenge liberals fearlessly but also rethink key propositions associated with the left during this phase when the movement was weak and had so little structure left on the ground in South Africa.

At the same time, there was a second scene in Oxford, which also included good seminars on southern Africa sometimes, above all at St Antony's, a wonderful community of interesting students from many countries, often aware of new intellectual tendencies spurred by the revival of an independent left. Again by dramatic contrast to Yale, I made many very good friends, a few of whom would be helpful to me in the future. Of those I didn't know well there were individuals about whom I read to this day as intellectual forces: the late Argentinian radical theorist Ernesto Laclau, Jonathan Israel, historian of the Enlightenment, Margaret Macmillan, who became warden of the college, Gabi Gorodetsky with his mastery of the Maxim Litvinov papers, and Sir Richard Evans, historian of Germany, whom I did know fairly well. These were just a few among a fairly small crew. But I should mention as well those who were important to my life.

Firstly, I was taken up by a small group of recent graduates of Magdalen College, Oxford. These included two historians, John Davis, an Italian specialist, and particularly Dick Miller, who wrote about Swiss anarchists but became in time an accountant. Through them I got to know the two other former college members, the art historians Malcolm Gee and John Gash, studying at the Courtauld Institute in London. Malcolm, a friend for life, eventually taught me how to understand modern art history in terms of markets and dealers, a field in which he was more or less the pioneer. Finally there was Innes Meek, who would become a fairly robust mainstream development person in the Commonwealth Development Corporation, the third generation in his family linked to Africa. These young men took me into their lives to the extent that I came to feel deeply at home with English people, admitted to their world.

Then there was a young woman who had done a degree at York University under Gwyn Williams, one of the first to bring Gramsci into the English-language discourse. Janet Jacobs was the daughter of a life-long working-class activist from the London East End, proud of having been expelled twice from the Communist Party. Janet wrote a brilliant thesis on worker history in pre-Communist times in Saint-Étienne, in France, with its old artisanal economy, but she could not abide the conventions of academic life and chucked it all in. She is a published poet, an enthusiastic walker and choir member, and still lives in the council flat where she grew up, just outside Regent's Park and its multi-million-pound Regency terrace houses. She has ever since been part of my life.

Through Janet (and beyond what I could figure out myself from staying in grotty rooms and student apartments), I started to develop a sympathetic understanding of the life of the English working class. Fiercely independent-minded, she was part of a movement of individuals, notably women, who profited from the extension of higher education bursaries to bright working-class individuals. Several others were also to become good friends of mine here and later in my Nigerian days. I should mention Diane Elson, the noted feminist economist, daughter of Midlands teachers who had also moved up from the working class and brought their daughter up in a left tradition. Diane was so kind as to start the uphill battle of explaining economics to me. The last name I must mention is that of Roger Brew, a student of Colombian economic development, who was to die at thirty-one from a brain tumour. Roger's background was Lancashire bourgeois, grammar school liberal, but his interest in industrialisation and economic development outside the West (his work is still sometimes cited since he was a pioneer of the history of modern Medellín in particular) attracted me very much and we were great friends.

This whole crew offered more to me as friends than people had since high school, a wonderful dense human network. It took a while to learn to function in this class-ridden world marred admittedly at times by hideous Industrial Revolution-era food and the absence of central heating, to which I became inured with some difficulty. But, on the other hand, there was the general friendliness of most English people and their surprising acceptance of me. England was also a great place for avant-garde music and art, and there was a buzzing world of far-left politics that carried into, for instance, the media, which won me over as a natural home.

There are also a few other South Africans I ought to mention who loomed large in this period and who were important in my formulation of an understanding of the country. Martin Legassick, whom I have already introduced, was a radical liberal who turned from a small underground cell to exile, first in the US and then in England, where he discovered Marxism – and I mean by that that he really knew his Marx. He exposed in his most powerful writing the extent to which the social system in South Africa resonated, not with backward Boers trekking ever further from civilisation, but with imperialism and the imperatives of big capital. He certainly could be difficult but he was a very loyal, kind friend who would play a somewhat bigger role in my life in time. His discontent with the US academic system (he was a lecturer at the University of California Santa Barbara campus when students burned down the Bank of America branch office) – plus the accident that he was very interested too in the early nineteenth-century Cape – made him a fortuitously blessed friend. I also must add to the list two other St Antony's students. Firstly, there was the immensely witty Sholto Cross. Sholto wrote a thesis on Zambia but he had been close to the ANC–SACP in exile. He became deeply disillusioned in Zambia both about Zambia and about the liberation movement without losing an essentially critical understanding of South African society (which he loved and to which he ultimately returned). He made it possible for me to grasp that one could be a radical, even a Marxist, without a religious devotion to black liberation politics. Also at St Antony's was a Swiss-educated Canadian, the urbane Rick Johnstone. I knew Rick and his wife very well from Cape Town, where we often hung out together. But Rick was the man who wrote a massively important book on the political economy of the gold mines and their centrality to the whole social and economic system. This was a masterly achievement, one of the high points of the new historiography of South Africa, and it pointed the way to the study of South African political economy, to which I have subscribed ever since. It is owing to Rick that any South African historian will now talk about the Mineral Revolution. As with Martin, Rick was far in advance of me and helped my development considerably. Neither Sholto nor Rick remained an academic with a South African focus for long. Rick was sufficiently unattracted to Communism to write a slightly strained comparative research paper comparing the gold mines in the Transvaal with the one at Kolyma developed with forced labour under very harsh conditions in Siberia. After that, living and working in Newfoundland, he turned, I believe, to ecology.

I also got to know very well a Rhodesian liberal, Tony Kirk, who used the chance to do an Oxford DPhil on South African history to mark a transition out of his doomed country. Tony was no Marxist ever, but he was both generous and highly intelligent, again defying the stereotype at a time when to be a white Rhodesian was to be a butt of the humour magazines par excellence in England. Tony had certainly got over Ian Smith, if ever he admired him, but he was involved in shadowy activities aiming at some kind of alternative solution. I should finally mention one historian who should have been in southern England but whom I knew from Yale, one of a few younger Africanists in Thompson's time whom I did befriend. This was David Yudelman, who wrote a fine book on the politics of white labour and the state in the 1920s and had a very antiseptic and thoughtful approach to this history – once again, someone who went far beyond the existing paradigms. David became a banker in Montreal after Yale, yet another interesting graduate student who parted ways in time with academe.

My time in England as well as in Africa in 1969–1970 was life-changing for me in a number of ways. The stimuli were now so many, so varied, so exciting, so apparently related to a changing world, that the milieu in which I grew up simply lost interest for me. By leaving the US, I gained entry to social groups that reflected what I was reading, what I was interested in professionally, my politics and also my ambitions and changing sense of identity. At the start of my trip abroad, I still had something in me of the American kid not used to foreign ways. By the end, I returned to Yale and found America strange and, to some degree, repellent. I was afflicted as well with acute Anglophilia.

The second feature of these years was more professional in kind. I started to figure out what sort of historian I wanted to be and how to take on Africa as subject matter. The third, related of course, involved developing a way of understanding South Africa. I certainly made many new contacts and friends in these years, now a cosmopolitan and very varied group who influenced me in many different directions. What they also revealed was my attraction to people who didn't 'fit in' and who had difficulties with dominant perspectives, academic rules and overly haughty senior figures.

Finally, in these years I broke, emotionally speaking, pretty permanently and decisively with the world I knew from the North Side of Chicago and notably from my family. In 1970 my much-loved and kindly grandmother Lucie Gross died of cancer. It was painful to see her become thinner and thinner, unable to do anything about this condition (although the stupid family idea was to keep me from this sight), and eventually she was gone at the age of eighty. My parents, with my father's love of saving money and the need to buy an apartment in Chicago that would avoid having to move on during the 'condo' craze, bought a tiny apartment with one bedroom in an Art Deco building to the north of our old neighbourhood. This was an area which was the centre of blight on the North Side. Their large building was well situated right against Lincoln Park but there was no commercial world around it whatsoever and it had a particular bleakness about it, despite being secure and well run. And it was cheap.

My parents were in no material need. When the Social Democrats returned to power in Austria in 1970, they decreed that 'involuntary emigrants' from the *Anschluss* years who had all the correct paperwork (and, of course, my parents both individually did) could collect their Austrian pensions at the age of sixty-five. Those already past that age, like my father, had to place a fixed but modest sum with the authorities and those under that age, like my mother, could simply start once again to contribute. Among the crowd of old Viennese in Chicago, little else was talked about for months. For some the benefits only came when the requirements were further loosened, but my parents both qualified immediately. My father, increasingly burdened at work as he aged, was delighted to quit. This money made quite a difference. It was substantially larger than the miserable US Social Security payments plus the small pensions my parents had as entitlements, and they did not pay any tax. In effect it guaranteed them a very nice long vacation every year, in alternate years going back at last to Europe and to the West Coast, taking in my uncle and aunt in San Francisco. Neither suffered from expensive ailments, so most of the money was left to me after my mother died. My parents always felt like Austrians; they would never say, 'the Austrians were like this, this is how they treated us'. We were them. There were good ones and not so good ones. And while hardly making up for the horrors of the Hitler years, the financial compensation was reconciliatory in its effect. If equivalent gestures had been made relatively soon after 1945, they might well have gone back to Austria, something they apparently had considered seriously.

There was no plan to include me in 5044 North Marine Drive 7D, and, for my father, the move symbolised quite plainly that I was going my own way. As a result, the tension that had existed between us from almost my earliest memories very gradually dissipated and, by the time he died (in 1989), had been replaced by a positively friendly connection admittedly with little direct communication. I like to think that I can now understand

Figure 7.1: My parents back in Austria, at Altaussee, 1975

the world a bit better as he saw it, unlike me as he was, and appreciate what was impressive about him.

This was not at all true of my mother. From her late fifties her hearing deteriorated and she was increasingly unwilling to admit this. She became very irritable and any communication with her became difficult. She turned into a kind of over-dependent, hysterical mother demanding contact but with little real affection – desperate phone calls to my friends if, for some reason, the post came a bit late and the like, as I once learnt. But there was no real relationship there anymore. At best it was rather nice to go to a concert with her; deafness or not, she still had a great feeling for classical music of the sort she admired. This was what remained of the intellectuality of her youth.

She had no interest at all in my adult life, how I lived or the people I knew. I suspect what always sat in her mind was that she deserved to have a dutiful son with a conventional family life and a comfortable income living close by to fit her needs. She didn't read my books or articles, she showed little belief in my ability to control my own life, and there was no pleasure in being with her, notably in this tiny confined apartment, which I would visit from time to time, that made no concessions to my needs. It was typical that in her last years, beyond expressing the desire for a visit on my part, she would try to insist on paying for it as though I could not afford to travel. She had no grasp of the notion that this might be humiliating as well as absurd. Perhaps she saw her well-to-do and apparently conventional nephews as a role model I ought to have followed. My relationship with my mother had been such a close one when I was a child and into my teens. Now when I think of her, I have occasional nightmares of being pushed away and feeling emotionally excluded. My visits to Chicago would become grudging and my best moments at the apartment were spent clutching my return ticket.

I may mention on a more casual note that I had two pleasant and quite memorable short-term living experiences with other families. In The Hague, I was taken into a Catholic Dutch family by a woman who ran her own printing business and was much interested (probably because of her divorce) in the new waves penetrating the church, notably in the Netherlands. I got used to pea soup, to plain yoghurt as a dessert, to *poffertjes* on the seaside at Scheveningen, and to St Nicholas' Day – and to everyday Dutch life. It was an important step in assimilating European ways.

In Cape Town I moved into the cottage of Joan Charlton, also a divorcee and, in some respects, typical of the wave of English immigrants attracted to the good life in South Africa after World War II. As her husband prospered, he found another and perhaps younger wife and moved up to Johannesburg. How could one leave Joan? She was such a liberal, observant, witty and intelligent person, admittedly with little formal education, and with quite a good and usually side-splitting take on white South African life. I found white South African society in 1969 stilted and old-fashioned on the whole. My fascination with it in macro terms was matched by an ability to relate only to a few marginal inhabitants on this first visit. Most of the South Africans I first came to like were those living far away from the country. Joan Charlton eventually returned to the bleak North Sea town of Lowestoft, where I once visited the family. She was eager to get her boys, the gay classical singer and the blond surfer, later to turn to photography, out of the country. This little cottage was located five minutes' walk from the beach road in Camps Bay. With the sweeping Atlantic on one side and the majestic Twelve Apostles rising next to Table Mountain behind, the beauty of this spot beat everything. I certainly thought this must be the most beautiful place to live. Of course, today Camps Bay is a very wealthy suburb, which it wasn't then. Both these households put my own background and family history into perspective.

I can also use the African trip to mention, finally, one political development that mattered to me. I deliberately chose to see Egypt, not just to enjoy its fabulous sights but also to have a glimpse of a radical nationalist regime. My main memory of Nasser's Egypt was the austerity and the virtual lack of a (for me) normal consumer culture. I found this sufficiently interesting to reinforce my alienation from Zionism. My father in Austria had been a keen Zionist, but for me Israel did not mean much. The only kin we had there (on my mother's side) were distant and not in contact with us. However, the sense of social experimentation and identification with an international left, which seemed to include Israel, was appealing so far as I knew in the days when I took Hebrew classes. In 1967 came the Six Day War when Israel gobbled up the so-called Occupied Territories, the remainder of Palestine left to Arabs twenty years before. This made me think about what Israel was really up to. Nothing in the discourse to which one was treated in Jewish circles suggested that there had remained a desire to take over this remaining space. Unlike in 1948, the Arab population of the West Bank and Gaza was now essentially left intact; they did not perhaps have the time to flee, so Israel was left with the problem of how to deal with this large element, unlike the relatively 'empty land' it inherited earlier when the Arab population largely fled. The response was jubilation at the full control of Jerusalem, which was now never to be returned, and an insistence that a withdrawal would only happen if the Israelis got what they wanted – full diplomatic recognition for themselves and the Arabs eating humble pie.

This, in fact, they got from Anwar Sadat after 1973, but otherwise the Israelis were faced with a long-term occupation which continues to the present. They were prepared neither to let go and lose the strategic advantage nor to incorporate, which meant becoming something other than the so-called Jewish state. I started to feel that this Jewish state stuff went smack against the principles I had about politics elsewhere and I became angry at having, in my view, been taken in by a questionable nationalist movement. In 1969 I thought of visiting Israel but was simply too exhausted as my big trip to Africa neared an end. (That was why I passed a few days in Cyprus, which in the end were spent on the beach in the Turkish zone at Kyrenia.) Later I simply wanted nothing to do with the place. When my parents went there, I probably didn't probe deeply enough what they thought. My mother located a once-Austrian second cousin and, through her, a once-Czech third cousin, but this contact was not continued and I suspect my mother's dislike of many Jewish associations and my father's attraction to some, but only some, aspects of them were not dispelled. There was never a question of a second trip. As for me, I suppose it has meant that I tend to try to find out, when I meet Jewish people, what they think of this wonderful homeland with which I have had very little to do.[2] I look askance at Jewish institutional life and I believe that in 1969 I learnt to avoid committing myself to a purely Jewish group in the interests of relating to a wider world.

8 | The Tough Years Begin

My *annus mirabilis* was certainly 1969. The world seemed an exciting place to be and I really enjoyed this phase of life; the year enormously enriched me and changed me. I thought this was the foundation of my future adult life and didn't heed how weak the material basis was for its continuation. Once I was back in New Haven, eager to write up my thesis and move on to a job as soon as possible, the curtain came down and the bad times essentially began. It would be many years before I woke up in the morning with a feeling of longer-term security.

There had been a couple of curtain-raisers. What were the warning signs? At some point in the spring of 1968, a visitor of some note whose specialty was Africa came to Yale. I got wind of this when favoured undergraduates were invited to meet him, but I was left out. I complained (to William Roger Louis, I think) and did get to attend the event, but in the end felt that what had happened was indicative of something I hadn't suspected and was not a good omen.

More to the point, that spring I failed my big oral exam. I had no idea what that exam would be like. I assumed it would be essentially factual and did not expect analytical questions that had no real connection with one another. I had never failed any sort of test in my life, so this came as a big shock. In order to move on and get on with research, I had to have a second go. For this I was better prepared and I have the slightly schlocky memory that someone was playing the Beatles' 'Hey Jude' when I was permitted to take a short break in the middle. I felt confident I was through, and indeed I was. Given Yale's generosity in supporting my research, I put this unpleasant story out of my memory.

The reality is that in the spring of 1970 I entered the academic job market assuming that a job would follow as smoothly as everything else had since I entered college, but this proved instead to be an absolute sticking point, which took over my life for many years, as if a dark cloud sat in the sky. I would ascribe this to three causes, and it is hard to know which was the most important.

The first was that African history had suddenly shifted from a field with a dearth of candidates to one where there was a small but growing glut. What interest there was, was mostly aimed at finding an acceptable black candidate, African or American, to meet the racial nationalist militancy which was threatening the liberal peace of colleges. In general, academic jobs, along with the economy more generally, were drying up at the time. Graduate school was not really, as I assumed, an apprenticeship to academic employment. I was faced with the reality that the institution that did have a job to offer would inevitably go for one individual only; it was a competition rather than a situation where one crossed a threshold and was admitted. The second reason was my lack of a patron. Swanson was off to Miami University of Ohio and made no further attempt to contact me. Leonard Thompson, who now took over, was interested solely in the advancement of Leonard Thompson and certainly not in me. The third was that my vision of things, my way of doing history and my politics did not fit Yale and did not fit the emerging dominant trends in African history. In the narrowing job market, this increasingly mattered. It was not that I got pipped at the post. I got nowhere: no nibbles, no interviews, nothing. This situation, so far as the US was concerned, continued uninterruptedly until I left for South Africa for good in 1984. Hundreds of letters were sent into space as the years went by. I did have work some of this time and some very interesting experiences, as we shall see, but the overall situation was, with varying degrees of intensity, persistently worrying.

In the end I found a solution but it left an intense bitterness in me. I sometimes wonder what I would have become if, as I thought would surely happen, I had obtained some modest tenured job in the US heartland, far away from any real African context. What I can say is that it would have made a considerable difference; it was in truth a road not taken and would have made for a different life. In my willingness to move very far from my roots, I was adventurous and willing to take a chance, but, as for being able to consider alternatives professionally, I knew really just enough to dig in my heels and carry on with whatever attracted me intellectually. And I was haunted by the feeling that, in general, friends and family saw me as good for nothing apart from this academic project. There was no faith, even on my part, that I could do something else, enjoy it and be good at it. This made the story a soul-destroying one for much of the time.

At the point where I finished a draft of my thesis, I still had enough confidence to want to head off from Yale to my happy English hunting grounds, where I could return to what mattered to me and to the people I had come to like there. The result was a prolonged and deeper acquaintance with the fragile life I was building for myself in England, but, with time, money ran out and I was finally forced to come back to Yale, to nothing. Leonard Thompson made some minor criticisms of the thesis and used them to demand a further revision and submission, putting his 'stamp' on it – another humiliation. He had no idea of what made my thesis interesting and how it worked. I survived in New Haven mostly thanks to a bit of money that Moore Crossey found to enable me to work in the library. Finally, in the autumn of 1971 my thesis was approved and I had the hollow reward of a PhD behind me. Moore's money was running out and the autumn was drawing to a close.

Then a break finally came. A small college in upstate New York wanted a one-term teacher of African history at the last moment. They asked me to come for an interview and I flew there. I remember my shock when arriving in Utica at discovering how cold it could get in November, even in my classy French leather coat. Kirkland College accepted me for this job, perhaps because David Miller, an earnest and avuncular Protestant, had known me very slightly at Yale and was part of the tiny History team, but mostly because there was a Yale connection. Someone had let them down, so they were fairly desperate for a qualified person to teach some history of the world outside the West. Kirkland was itself an unusual venue and it was an interesting and innovative time in the history of American higher education, so I need to describe this institution in some detail.

To do so, I turn to the memoirs of Kirkland College's one and only president, Sam Babbitt, who served from 1965, when the college began, to 1978, when it closed its doors.[1] I also need to explain to non-Americans that Kirkland belonged to the large number of small liberal arts private colleges offering only a first degree that flourished particularly in post-World War II America. These colleges had often been created to serve the needs of some particular religious denomination in some particular town or region, since they were mainly situated outside the cities, but, as they became secularised, they were also able to offer a sense of distinction (in Bourdieu's meaning of the word) and appeal to an affluent middle class looking for a safe environment and personal attention for their offspring.

The oldest such college in New York State west of the Hudson River valley was Hamilton College in the town of Clinton. Hamilton gradually developed into a college for men only, with a little under a thousand students (less than half the size of even the undergraduate portion of the University of Chicago) and it appealed to some well-to-do families in New York City as well as the business elites of the small towns and cities upstate. Its graduates tended to head towards Wall Street or towards business and professional lives in those cities. The tenured faculty stayed around for most of their lifetime, were a major factor in the life of the small local community, and offered much personal attention to interested students.

The relative isolation of Hamilton meant that there was growing discomfort with its all-male student body intake. The chief administrators became aware that it was losing out in the competition for admissions to other institutions that were coeducational and more urban in location. In the early 1960s the idea of integrating Hamilton in gender terms met with a conservative reaction, especially since the major universities that were, in respect of their undergraduates, single-sex institutions, such as Yale and Princeton, were still some years from taking this big step. The proposed solution was to found a women's college across the road from Hamilton as a companion institution.

Kirkland liked to call itself 'innovative'. It breathed the spirit of the 1960s too, not utterly unlike the University of Chicago, but the innovation lay not in a new political outlook but in curricular modernisation that made it somewhat different from the classic women's colleges of East Coast America, such as Vassar or Bryn Mawr. Kirkland cross-registered with Hamilton and offered new subject matter such as history of science, dance, fine arts and (surprisingly) sociology. The residences (some lovely modern buildings were created *de novo* in a patch of forest) were open – no prissy chaperones. Classes were small, often tiny, and students were not necessarily graded. They evaluated you and you evaluated them. As a teacher, you were expected to innovate all the time with new classes (based on a progressive set of readings, as was typical in American colleges). It may be interesting to reproduce a directive from 1964 to give the flavour of what was intended:

(1) To produce a woman who enjoys the process of learning in whatever situation life places her.
(2) To educate a wife able to share fully the experience of an educated husband in such a way that she grows with him while inspiring her children.
(3) To encourage women to regard themselves as fully capable to act in society by teaching them what women have done to meet the needs of society in ways that are beyond the abilities of men.
(4) To give women both the academic tools and the necessary confidence to carry on careers appropriate to the varying stages of their lives before marriage, on a part-time basis during motherhood and on a full-time basis after their children are grown.[2]

If we look at the history of feminism over the past half-century, the way women see themselves and are depicted has evolved quite fast and goes so far beyond these directives that they now seem quaint, even as advice intended for girls from affluent families and (very often) private schools. According to current ideas, women need rather the competitive experience to go out and get the same professional training and career habitus that men are supposed to have. They need entrée into the worlds of architecture, medicine, law and science, which are inevitably joined to full-time careers, awkward as that may be for many in the US particularly, given the lack of state intervention to help with childcare and other forms of traditionally female obligations. Kirkland simply did not begin to have the resources to make this possible and so fit the world that started to open up quite rapidly. By 1975 a survey indicated that 'very few of our students had chosen Kirkland because it was a college for women'.[3] There were a diminishing number of takers for what seemed to be 'innovative' and on offer a decade earlier. Indeed, the appeal of the college was increasingly the good academic standards of Hamilton.

To his liberal credit, Babbitt twice pointed out in his memoir the disquiet of key Hamilton figures at the number of Jews in the faculty and student body of Kirkland.[4] He never refers in his memoir to the fact that the college 'bought in' to some scholarship programme or programmes so that the girls would not be lily-white. The black students, many of whom I taught (there were no black teachers), had no interest in the Kirkland idea whatsoever and, without this orientation, also struggled to survive with decent pass marks. They were a small and inevitably unhappy little brood that stuck together and only a few did enough to get a degree. By contrast, the black boys at Hamilton were more likely to have selected Hamilton. There were only a few but they were far more competent students. Still, I had the experience, renewed years later at Harvard, of being accepted by black youth but in an exhausting and difficult environment where tension prevailed in the classroom between the two 'races', tension that had to be assuaged with classes orchestrated deliberately to that end.

Babbitt was a great representative of the old liberal end of the American elite. He had been a student of something called American studies at Yale, a kind of amalgam of intellectual history and literature. Whatever the achievements of American studies – and several other teachers at Kirkland could be associated with it – it was hardly a solid foundation for the intellectual life of this college. It struggled to maintain the number of good students applying to it and Babbitt faced a constant challenge in raising money. Hamilton was not a college that changed quickly, but it did change and, with time, the admission of significant numbers of qualifying Jews and, more to the point, the admission of girls, following the model of the big Ivy League men's colleges, became more and more acceptable. To Babbitt's chagrin, Hamilton foreclosed and Kirkland was incorporated into it, by which time I was long gone.

I was thrilled initially when I got the job at Kirkland, especially as it coincided with the acceptance for publication of my earliest articles (there were three or four on early South African society before I left), and in the end I stayed in Clinton for two years, although in the final semester I lived off unemployment insurance and had no work. There was always the threat of being thrown out of academic life hanging over me, with little sense of any possible alternative.

I would say that Kirkland had an important influence on me since, being thrown in at the deep end, I learnt to be a good teacher to good students especially if I could find the right wavelength, learnt to speak well, to mark papers fairly, to encourage talent and to interact effectively with many of them. This part I enjoyed thoroughly and these lessons served me well for all my life, as did the great general background I got in the classics from the University of Chicago and my wide range of reading. As an example, I can cite the chance of teaching an independent course on the history of anarchism (I had by now read a lot of left history writing) to the two bright children of America's hottest academic writers on sex: Masters and Johnson. I still recall with pleasure that nice wad of marijuana that these two delightful kids gave me as a present at the end. Indeed, through my student Hildy Armour, I got to know a group of undergraduates with whom I often hung out. I made friends as well with the two or three young bachelors who taught at Kirkland. It made for a nice time and it was my most intense experience of WASP America, for once with no little group of Jewish intellectuals as a ground platform. Maybe half my students were boys; I had no problem in sidestepping the feminist creed in this way and got to know some of the male students as well as the female.

In this autobiography, I haven't had a chance to talk about my growing affection for natural beauty. The earliest strong memory of this was very early indeed: the trip to visit my aunt and uncle in San Francisco when I was just shy of three years (in April 1947). In the dreary environs of the north side of Chicago, my memory of the California poppies, the hummingbirds, the hills, all the beautiful things of the Bay Area, lasted many years. Of our family vacations, all of which I liked, my favourite by far (I must admit, with the added advantage of my father being left out) was Colorado. I learnt to love to hike and to enjoy high mountain scenery. Obviously New York State cannot compete with the High Rockies. However, it too is beautiful, and here I lived outside any city for two solid years.

I remember walks in the woods and the trees turning afire with blood orange and carmine red in the autumn, especially when driving up into the Adirondack Mountains. I remember picking up fresh non-alcoholic apple cider for sale in season, rafting with my Hamilton College psychologist friend Larry Finison, experiencing the beautiful long winters with fresh clean snow and bright blue skies, becoming interested in ice hockey and watching Hamilton games. I lived above an antiques store in an early nine-teenth-century building where supposedly one of America's least mem-orable presidents, Millard Fillmore, last chief executive from the Whig Party, had once been a schoolmaster – actually, a very unlikely idea. This in turn was located on a lovely square which had a church or two and the college inn on its sides. From the square, a road went up the hill to the two colleges. I very much enjoyed the routines and feeling part of an America (a bit distressingly conservative part) that I knew almost entirely from books.

Nonetheless, when I looked back I realised that, without a wife, life in this picture-book backwater would have become lonely and perhaps peculiar. I had seen Edward Albee's *Who's Afraid of Virginia Woolf?* and its mordant and unforgettable picture of life for long-time denizens of a small college. Could I have developed as an intellectual? What would I do for company once I was clearly too old for the students? If I found a student I really liked, why would she want to stay in Clinton, New York? Nonetheless, my sense of depression was intense indeed when I had to move on from this lovely little place to, as far as I was concerned, nothing – the third and last return to New Haven. Moore Crossey was taking leave

Figure 8.1: My home at 8 East Park Row, in the town square of Clinton, New York, where I lived upstairs above an antiques store, 1972–1973

for a research project, and so I was able to work in the University Library as his replacement for a few months. I drove my orange Datsun (Hildy taught me to drive a stick shift car) out of town on a dreary winter morning and I never returned.

The first half of 1974 comprised arguably the most miserable months of my life. I like old towns and I did not dislike New Haven, which, now that I owned a car, I could explore a bit more. However, returning in this way to almost nothing was awful. I made the mistake, until the spring, of boarding with the mother of a Kirkland student. Being naturally very messy although an increasingly adept cook, I horrified this tidy divorcee with my ways and it was unpleasant driving down to the shore and feeling anything but at home after a workday ended. Fred Cooper continued to be great company but he was now heading for a first job at the University of Michigan, and even before that materialised, he had ideas about what else he could do with his life if need be. All I had was my mother's (and thus much-resented) standby idea of working in a library. Still, I applied to and got into the library graduate programme of the State University of New York at Albany (since I qualified as a New York resident) and thought, if all else failed, this could be my next step. I did take pride in being asked by the Yale University Library to identify what had been drawn on an eighteenth-century map and, with a bit of reconnoitring and by process of elimination, I could say that it was a map of the coast of India with the various European forts and enclaves depicted. I got a nice letter of thanks and it made me feel a bit less useless.

One evening, eating a pizza in Wooster Square, the core Italian neighbourhood of New Haven (actually a city with a very high percentage of ethnic Italians), I poured out some of my frustration and humiliation to a group of fellow or previous graduate students. To Henry Abelove,[5] I owe the advice that probably took me to my next phase of life. Henry said that I must discard all my letters of recommendation from the file and replace them, and indeed I could by then replace them with letters from Kirkland. At first this seemed like strange advice since the Kirkland people knew little of my intellectual interests or my writing, but I had nothing to lose and I followed it up. Among the advertisements to which I responded, there were international positions on offer, including some for African universities, although by this time African countries on the whole were replacing their expatriates with locals. Next thing I wrote to a Nigerian university by chance and, to my astonishment, I got a nice letter from a professor named Bob Gavin asking for more details about me, which I proceeded to provide.

Was it Henry's advice that saved the day? Some years later, when I had a chance to peek into the files and actually saw my letters from Kirkland, I was struck by how lukewarm they were, especially given the effusiveness that usually marks academic recommendation letters in American graduate schools. Still, they may have sounded good enough to foreigners, and who knows what a Swanson or a Thompson would have produced?

Then, well into the spring of 1974, as I was packing late one warm afternoon to drive to New York where Tom Leighton, now living on Tompkins Square,[6] was awaiting me for the weekend, the doorbell rang. By the time I got to the door, the delivery man was gone, but there was a telegram notification in the box. I thought about that job in Nigeria, and decided to call Tom and prolong my stay in New Haven until I could fetch the telegram (it was Friday) in person after another hour or so. I drove to Western Union and, to my uncontained joy, there was indeed a telegram offering me a two-year contract to teach history at Ahmadu Bello University in the city of Zaria. My academic career was saved.

When my little job at the library came to an end, I headed my Datsun westwards and spent a frustrating summer in Chicago waiting for a Nigerian visa, which was not necessarily a certainty. Gradually the last of my saved money was all spent. And then one day the visa came. Off I went, back to London once again and then onwards, by what would become the familiar air route from Gatwick to Kano on a British Caledonian flight. I arrived to sunshine, heat and the beginnings of the harvest, and there was Uba, the department driver, waiting as scheduled to take me on the two-hour drive to Zaria, with which I would also become very familiar.

9 | An Intellectual and an African: Nigeria

In order to make sense of this part of my life, I need to say a bit about Northern Nigeria and the society in which I was about to live for four formative years. Centuries before, this relatively well-watered and populous part of the West African savanna evolved a hierarchical multitude of mud-walled towns in which rulers, cognisant of Islam through trade, gradually adopted this sophisticated religion as a legitimating device as well as continuing to patronise older beliefs. At the start of the nineteenth century, a Muslim teacher initiated a spectacular series of jihads that expanded the writ of a more orthodox Islam and diffused Islamic culture especially in the towns, which were now graced with palaces and mosques. Kano became a great trading centre with North and North-East Africa; North Africa was clearly the model of progress. The overrule of the jihad centre of Sokoto was mostly accepted by the towns, including my new home of Zaria, well to the south of both Sokoto and Kano. This was a part of Africa that experienced an important developmental thrust. The Hausa language started to be written extensively in Arabic script; commerce and even craft manufacture flourished; a kind of bureaucracy developed. The British conquest occurred only after 1900, so the entire colonial period lasted just sixty years, really just a person's lifetime, and the system of indirect rule, for which Northern Nigeria was a model in Africa, at least meant that 'native' rulers with their retinues were propped up – assuming good behaviour – and the British presence was actually very limited.

Much of the economy, which featured wealthy merchants, remained outside European hands entirely, although peanuts and to some extent cotton were cultivated for export. Slavery, which had been very prevalent, gradually faded away. For me, an enjoyable aspect of daily life and of bigger trips involved visiting markets and admiring handicrafts and cloth for sale as well as gauging something of how people lived and interacted.

Northern Nigeria consisted of more than the related series of Hausa-speaking emirates. Not only did the countryside bear signs of an older culture (though much less by my time) but there were many areas, notably on high ground, difficult to control with cavalries, that continued to be inhabited by small, varied language groups, many dozens in fact. They had escaped the control of the Muslim cities. Moreover, it included areas south of the jihad-influenced world as well. Inhabitants of the Jos Plateau in the east-centre of the North spoke some seventy languages, and there were other small ethnic groups near the border with Cameroon. Then there was the 'Middle Belt', which bordered the two southern regions. I mention this particularly because the majority of our students were from these minority areas, which had been enthusiastically, even quite fanatically, Christianised by determined Protestant missionaries. The minorities were particularly important because they were often very oriented to European-style education. By contrast, the emirates people were suspicious of the new Western schools, although the British did create a small secular system to cater to an elite group. Despite a few impressive individuals normally from leading families, the emirates were very far behind educationally, and dramatically behind the southern part of Nigeria, to which they were joined for reasons that mostly made sense in broader British colonial strategy.

When Nigeria became independent, it did so as a federal republic with three units. This proved highly unstable and led to the outbreak of civil war in 1966, partly motivated too by the discovery of massive oil reserves, which came to enrich the state enormously. The Biafran War and its aftermath were still something to talk about in 1974. Much of the population in Zaria undoubtedly remembered the massacres of Southerners in the town and on the campus, as elsewhere in the North, which had taken place only eight years earlier and which had helped precipitate the war. By my time there were twelve states, and the president of the republic, Yakubu Gowon, educated by Christians in Zaria, was a Middle Belter. For many purposes, citizenship in Nigeria hinged on one's state of ancestry, not merely of birth, and this remains true, still bedevilling national unity to the present. The 1973 war in the Middle East had led to a large hike in

Figure 9.1: Jibiya market, near Nigeria's northern border with Niger, 1976

the price of oil, the commodity that was coming to dominate the Nigerian economy. As a result the government coffers were full, the naira was strong and, to an extent, convertible, reconstruction was very well under way, and the university seemed to have big resources.

The picturesque walled city of Zaria was the seat of an emir and the site of what was often considered the most impressive of all nineteenth-century mosques. It was also an important rail junction and its location on the railway line had brought in numerous foreigners. In effect there were several units forming the city that were still poorly integrated. Outside the partly decaying mud walls of the city, there was the Government Residential Area, or GRA, with colonially built bungalows and a couple of shops (Indian and Lebanese) where expatriates did most of their daily commercial transactions. There was also a special area demarcated for non-Muslim Nigerians and another for Muslims who were not Hausa. Some miles away was Samaru, where the massive university grounds were located. The landscape was largely flat, but here and there were big rock formations and typically, as in Kano, a great hill, which no doubt had had sacral as well as defensive significance long ago. A sacred pool was rumoured to have once been the site of human sacrifices. There was red earth-yielding sand everywhere, as if the whole Sahara had blown in, and it appeared to dominate especially in the long bone-dry season. Eventually the dry weather became hotter and hotter and more humid until finally the rains broke and brought good precipitation for four to five months of the year.

This was not a society that easily allowed the penetration of outsiders, to put it mildly. In the traditional Hausa compound, for instance, the first entrance, perhaps supervised by some minor client of the household, was the *zaure*. And that is as far as anyone but close friends of the family could go. My new Sudanese colleague, Professor Ismail, liked to say that Islam (which was not identical to Hausa culture) was not exclusively a religion but a way of life, and its different elements – female seclusion, clothing preference, prayer five times a day, eating prohibitions and so on – marked this boundary between insiders and outsiders constantly. I found it

Figure 9.2: A durbar in Zaria, 1975

easier to understand this, having been brought up as a Jew, because, while American Jewish life had secularised and had more or less ceased being that kind of way of life for the great majority, the old system about which you could read and which still exhibited traces, the old customs, were not much different from those among Muslims through the long centuries. They certainly followed the same basic idea of integrating identity, belief and culture. Jews were different in that it had long since been made clear to them that proselytising outsiders was forbidden territory, whereas for Muslims this was a prime duty. Some of my Christian colleagues were certainly more alienated by, and even hostile to, Islam and its ways than I was. It took a long while to make new friends in this world, and in general ordinary people were much happier with you if you learnt Hausa (mine was very basic at best) and became Muslim yourself, the mark of civilised behaviour.

Ahmadu Bello University (ABU), named after the first caliph appointed after the great wave of religious war and renewal, had become by 1974 the biggest university in Nigeria. During my four years, there was, apart from the main Zaria campus, a branch at Kano, much smaller but eventually a separate university. There were also more distant branches of Southern universities at Ilorin and Jos, still quite new. The oldest institution of higher education, in Ibadan, dated back to 1948 and set a template for late-colonial reform and was still just about the apex of the educational system. Yet ABU had grown and clearly was favoured by the central state. As already mentioned, a large part of the student body was not made up of Hausa first-language-speaking Northerners but came from minority ethnic groups in good part belonging to the ten per cent of the Northern population that counted themselves as Christians.

Of the Nigerians on the faculty, the striking feature was the relative absence of Southerners. There was clearly an intention to exclude them from a situation where they could easily become the dominant element until Northerners could fill the desired spots. Moreover, the faculty included members of the real elite of the North from the ex-emirates (which still had some local governmental power) and they were obviously the 'heirs apparent' to power in the institution.

We had only one Southerner in the large and well-supplied History Department, Joe Inikori, now of the University of Rochester in the US, but there were half a dozen Westerners and several other foreigners. In fact, there were many, many *Turawa* (Europeans) at the university. Awash as the country was with oil wealth, far more in Nigeria than there had ever been in colonial times, they were involved in a great variety of projects but were notably to be found at the newer universities that had sprung up. There were hundreds at ABU, almost all on contracts, and they formed a community unto themselves or, indeed, quite a few interlocked communities. The university had a distinct and well-established Institute of Agricultural Research in what was, after all, the age of the Green Revolution in India, and there one found Americans living literally in houses shipped in with all their contents from the US Midwest – civilisation. This is not to speak of the numerous Asians, citizens of other African countries, and other individuals.

Moving into my work environment, I found myself part of a history department that was small compared with that at Yale but large compared with those of either Kirkland College or a South African university. My Western colleagues were a very mixed bag. Ian Linden was a very clever liberal Englishman converted into an enthusiastic Catholic, who had already written a few books on Rwanda and Malawi. In my memory, his Islamophobia could be vociferous.

Hans-Heino Kopietz was born in German-occupied Poland during the war and spent a refugee childhood in poor health in West Germany, followed by translation to a conservative corner of southern California where his mother, a nurse, had settled. In his own words, he was transformed from a juvenile delinquent into an enthusiastic student of history and politics in junior college. The teacher who inspired him, as we discovered one day when looking at letters from America, was none other than Jim Inskeep, my equally inspiring history teacher from Lake View High School, with whom Heino kept in contact – a remarkable coincidence. Jim had moulded these two members of a university history department thousands of miles away from his classroom. From Bakersfield Junior College, Heino went on to UCLA, where he became fascinated with the Middle East, and then the American University of Beirut. By the time I knew him, he was a divorced PhD student at the School of African and Oriental Studies (SOAS) in London, a place which had already made a deep impression on me. Our Muslim colleagues looked on Heino with the greatest suspicion as an overly Eurocentric teacher of the Middle East. I can remember an evening with Heino and Ian, as well as Bob Shenton, when I could finally celebrate those Marines evacuating the last Yankees by helicopter from the embassy in Saigon in 1975. Politically speaking, that was perhaps the happiest day of my whole life.

Third in the department came another Californian, the former Inez Jarrick, also a product of UCLA and SOAS, a nice plump liberal Jewish woman who, in the course of time spent in Tanzania, had hooked up with one of the four Johns that Terry Ranger brought together in the path-setting History Department of the University of Dar es Salaam: Johns Lonsdale, Iliffe, McCracken and Sutton. John Sutton was the archaeologist and he was attached to a research unit in Zaria, not to our department. He was a somewhat self-effacing, bush-loving and seemingly rather old-fashioned Englishman, albeit with a shrewd understanding of many aspects of African society. Inez also had eyes watching what she did as she taught southern African history. Then there was Bob Gavin, our head of department, a British historian of colonial Aden who had a French wife.

In addition to this crew, I should mention two other Westerners. The first is my friend Charles Stewart. I suspect Charles, a student of Thomas Hodgkin, remembered me from Oxford, where we were acquainted, and singled me out to Gavin as an applicant. So perhaps he saved me from becoming a New York State librarian. Charles, normally at the University of Illinois, was on long leave in Zaria. He was a real Islamicist, who wrote an interesting book on the scholar-tribesmen of the Mauritanian desert. This was far from my interests, but Charles was a kind and experienced observer, a fairly anglicised American also from the vicinity of Chicago, who taught me the ropes to a large extent and normally dispensed excellent advice. His wife, Elizabeth, also taught in the department at the same time. None of these people, however, except perhaps for John Sutton, succeeded in doing any significant research in Nigeria. Our generous vacation allowance and salaries also encouraged us to wander off when a break came and gave us a chance to leave behind the practical difficulties of life in Nigeria.

There were quite a few Westerners who passed through Zaria as researchers or spent time there, but one had a great influence in my life: Bob Shenton. Bob was a working-class boy from New Jersey who enthused about Marxism and loved big ideas about imperialism, underdevelopment and relations between Africa and Europe. His father was an immigrant from Britain. Like me, he was fascinated with Nigeria but uncomfortable with fitting into the world of the old Africa hands.

Bob had started out studying at Columbia but, in good part to evade the draft, went to the University of Toronto instead. He came to Nigeria with a young Canadian wife, but this marriage quickly dissolved. He had poor relations with Paul Lovejoy, the ambitious and prolific scholar of slavery, also an American based in Toronto, and our first intense times together came when Bob needed to walk out on Paul and find a place to stay and someone to talk to. My little flat contained a second bedroom that I could spare. So we both were outsiders to genteel American middle-class culture (as my Kirkland days hopefully demonstrate), we had drunk deep of the American youth culture of the sixties, we were very hostile to the war government in Washington, and we were also looking for a new way to write about West African history. For Bob, moving into the work which eventually led to an excellent thesis and book on capitalism and the early colonial system in the North was a struggle that involved intense talk, and the sharing of ideas and books. Eventually he became the first person with whom I ever co-authored a piece. And he stayed in Nigeria virtually as long as I did, securing a job after a while in the pre-university history programme at the School of Basic Studies.

Bob inspired me to write, for the very first time, a little piece on contemporary Nigeria that tried to pull the curtain from, rather than celebrate, the oil boom, which was having a drastically distorting effect on many aspects of development in the country. It was accepted, apparently not without controversy, by the *Review of African Political Economy*. He also convinced me to 'come out' as a Marxist, that the important thing was to write as one believed. I suppose I don't always do this, but I started to do so and nailed my colours to the Marxist mast for many years thereafter. And there is, of course, an emotional core to this, and it is still not dead in me. As the US Communist Party song says, 'Well, you ain't done nothing if you ain't been called a Red.' That still resonates for me, whether or not it makes the best sense to stand up all the time, and it goes back to my undergraduate days, although I am really concerned here to focus critically on the rationale of socialism, not its gut appeal to the senses.

While others taught African-related subjects, for me Marxism meant increasingly the study of Marx's understanding of capitalism in its generative form. But it is noteworthy that I have an historian's Marxism. This historical way of understanding economic change, and notably the idea of distinct modes of production that led to very different political and social outcomes, seemed to me powerful. I went slowly through *Capital* and carried on into the *Grundrisse* and other texts. Eric Hobsbawm, whom I admired from my first university class in history, was one of a limited number of trained historians who addressed Marxist theory. I think Marxism does look a bit different when seen through the eyes of an historian.

In my view, Marx writing about politics was, by contrast, a shrewd and impressive journalist who was essentially a creature of his own time. His hopes for a world without capitalism were not based on more than a partial insight into the great modern political forces of the last two centuries. While Marx provided us with a coherent and very insightful view of class, class politics only occasionally and partly developed as he hoped and predicted. Again very insightful is the writing by eminent Marxists on the imperialism of pre-World War I Europe. However, imperialism was in fact a contradictory force with many particularities, varying from place to place and time to time. Was it better for Africa to be developed on capitalist lines or to be exploited in crude, direct and limited ways? There is no simple answer borne out in all historical situations. The first imperialist force in Europe, Portugal, entered contemporary history as one of the poorest countries on the continent. India, once a colony 'drained' of wealth by British colonialism according to the first Marxist commentators, has actually become a major force in the capitalist world, as indeed Marx himself expected could happen. I was quick to find the idea that European capitalism required African servitude in order to 'develop' simplistic and limited, if not entirely wrong. This contradiction was manifest in the impetus and constraints of post-World War II development planning in colonialism's last flowering.

In two ways, moreover, the construction of socialism as a real alternative to capitalism seems to encounter huge obstacles. The first is that capitalism does sustain, despite ongoing crises, a dynamism through its competitive structuration which makes it conducive to creating new products through the application of human intelligence. It is hard to imagine abandoning it entirely for long. Such crises are inherent, I think, as Marx wrote. It may be that eventually, and perhaps with environmental issues taking the front stage, capitalism will implode. If there is an answer, and that is the second issue, it will require a strong response from an effective state, especially given the complexities of the global economy, rather than the democratic deliberation of socialist-inclined individuals and cooperatives. I have little to offer as to where this should leave socialists, beyond fighting for reforms, including those with counter-systemic intents, and trying to defend modifications to the capitalist system that are in place, though increasingly challenged by so-called neo-liberalism. Constructing a vision of a different world is also valuable. I am not very comfortable with American liberalism, but European social democracy is something which I can live with, defend and wish to take further.

I did not take seriously the idea of a Marxist revolution on my own block, and I was far less engaged in the story of Communist parties. Communism for an American by the 1970s was simply a non-starter nor was I very interested in being bound by the discipline of any political party. These seemed irrelevant to the Western world in which I lived.

Probably the writers who most influenced me in considering the Soviet Union were E.H. Carr on the economic side and, above all, Isaac Deutscher. My own maturing view was that there was much to be admired and wondered at in the Bolshevik Revolution and the world of the old Bolsheviks, and yet they represented only a small sliver of the early twentieth-century Russian people. Despite this, Lenin and his cohorts were determined to stay in power and, as a result, resorted to ruthless behaviour towards their enemies, foreign and local, and even to rivals on the left. They believed in the moral rectitude of their cause. At a tremendous cost, they succeeded. Stalin presided over the rise of new Bolsheviks, people from modest backgrounds suspicious of foreigners, suffused with Russian nationalism, and indifferent or hostile to avant-garde ideas, but urbanised, educated up to a point with a strong emphasis on technology, and formed by the system to which they were in key respects loyal. They created a society which moved ahead rapidly to industrialise. This new world had almost no contemporary equivalent: ensuring low levels of inequality, tying the huge Russian landmass together, diffusing education and health services, creating modern towns, and forming a military that in the end was crucial in defeating Hitler. Moscow was unwilling to contemplate the breakaway of the non-Russian outer parts of the old empire, but it is also true that they were ruled in such a way that some would have a higher living standard than Russia proper and all would be given some or other industrial function to perform. This was very unlike Western colonialism. The relationship with the so-called satellite countries occupied by the Red Army in 1944–1945 was rather different and, in most cases, bitterly resented after time.

The other side of the coin was, of course, the cruelty of the deeply illiberal measures Stalin took to eliminate potential and actual dissidents, to order people around and shut down private farming at a time of famine and at the cost of many lives – in effect, the creation of a brutal police state characterised by large-scale killings. Labour sites like Norilsk and Kolyma were often set up in extremely harsh environments. These habits took their toll still well after Stalin's death although the worst did not continue. There is nothing appealing for me in a socialism following in the footsteps of the Bolsheviks as a whole, but that does not mean that the Communist era was entirely negative or that there is nothing to be learnt from it. Any learning to be had is probably almost entirely in the broad sphere of economic and social development rather than in the liberatory promise of socialism.

As I have said, my explorations in the new US historiography convinced me that the Soviet 'empire' was essentially security-dominated and defensive rather than expansive. I continued to feel hostile to Western Cold War policies. It seemed a shame to me that Labour in Britain and other socialist or quasi-socialist formations didn't try to form a bridge between America and the Soviet Union, rather than signing up for NATO. In this I suppose I recapitulated the old Austrian socialist ideas with which my parents had grown up. I certainly could grasp the appeal of the Communist model for what we were starting to call the Third World.

I did think that Nigeria, where Communism was written about as though the politicians might one day just decide over a drink to opt for it when the mood took them, could have used some of this Bolshevik medicine. Bob in particular pushed me in the direction of reading authors such as Laclau, Wallerstein, Frank and Amin (this last the best of the bunch), suggesting radical ways of understanding economic development in the modern era. In some respects, I found this analysis powerful and appropriate to understanding West Africa. Certainly I got excited about the issues that they raised. However, I also kept my own judgement about Nigeria. I would say that the extremely patrimonial state, mired in corruption and only casually interested in 'development' beyond what it meant in the attainment of international muscle, had to be assessed in its own right. As Chinua Achebe so memorably indicated in *No Longer at Ease*, its problems could not be reduced to a foreign conspiracy. Big 'imperialist' rip-offs there were, but they reflected Western cynicism about Nigeria's rulers, and the new rich were hardly innocents. The imperialists and the Third World elites were partners who needed one another.

As sub-Saharan Africa went and still goes, Nigerian society has more of the making of a potentially dynamic capitalism than any of the other ex-colonies. It has no lack of 'entrepreneurship' and democracy is skin-deep; Nigerians tend to do what their ethnic and religious brokers require them to do. It is the dysfunctional state and the lack of a sense of public service, as Peter Ekeh wrote (I only discovered him much later), which have so far set the country back. Ekeh wrote elegantly about Nigerians forming two publics, one the national public and the other the ethnic entity. So I continued to play with ideas about African states, politics and social practices. Unlike many Marxists, I still admire the work of cultural interpreters such as Jean-François Bayart and, like even fewer, I refused to blame continental problems on 'imperialism' and foreign exploitation as the prime engine.

In general, I became more at home with Marxist concepts and language; this became my intellectual home. Bob Shenton and I experienced good times, happy times and bad times in the four years in Zaria and helped each other cope in our differently administered jobs. To some extent, the ties with Bob reminded me of the close ties in my New Haven days with Fred Cooper, from whom I learnt so much, but Bob was probably closer to me as an intellectual as well as in sharing the many difficult times that living in Nigeria entailed.

There were other signal friendships too. After the strains of the previous years and given my nature, I wanted to enjoy having a real job with a decent income, but making myself comfortable in this setting, finding the things I needed for practical living, took up much time and kept me inevitably in close social touch with the expatriate world. I should mention as an example that I did not abandon my wider intellectual interests. I became very friendly with a remarkable innovative crew of British teachers of drama who built the mud theatre in Zaria where I witnessed

Figure 9.3: Reunion with Bob Shenton and Tony Humphries, 1993

Athol Fugard's *Sizwe Banzi Is Dead* and other captivating performances. This followed from my moving into a little late-colonial bungalow whose other half was inhabited by Susannah and Brian Crow. Brian, one of the Drama people who would one day head the department at the University of Birmingham, and Tony Humphries, who would get a job in the British Foreign Office and earn an OBE, have remained friends for life.[1] Indeed, my list of English friends grew quite a bit in consequence of the days in Zaria.

On the Nigerian side, there are also many characters to mention, but I am not sure they individually had enough influence on my own life for me to write interestingly about them here. The student body we had was reasonable in size. Perhaps thirty history graduates finished each year, about two for each member of staff. Very few Nigerian students came into the

Figure 9.4: My cottage and trusty Renault, Zaria, 1978

Figure 9.5: The Drama Department at Ahmadu Bello University tries to make folktales come alive, 1976

university directly from school. Usually they first taught, went to teachers college and perhaps to the university School of Basic Studies. By the time they came to us, they were usually no longer that young and often had families to support. From their senior-year essay on, the core experience for them was generally to research and write on the place from where, and the people from whom, they came. This could lead to very original and interesting research, but it hardly taught them much about understanding the wider world, and it was subtly iniquitous in undermining any sense of identity as Nigerians as opposed to developing into representatives of and maybe future spokesmen for the Birom or the Tiv or the Igala or the Hausa of one emirate or another.[2] There was also a shadowy world of patronage where one offered a helping hand to another, to which the expatriates were relatively oblivious.

Also shadowy was the presiding head of the Northern History Research Scheme, a late-colonial creation, H.F.C. (Abdullahi) Smith. Smith, who had initially come out to work in the Sudan, belonged to the genre of late-colonial liberal reformist academics who took to the African country where they found themselves, married locally and stayed on after independence. Such people were typically fonts of local knowledge. John (Yunusa) Lavers, who headed our branch department in Kano, was another such man. Smith had married a Hausa woman and converted to Islam, and he stayed on until the end of his life in 1984. Unlike others, he brought a remarkable and original sense of Nigerian history to life in his few publications and also in his teaching. He went far beyond the story of the jihads in search of the history of material and cultural life as well as beyond the ethnic antecedents of current identities. My Nigerian colleagues certainly all knew him, but he rarely came to Zaria, holed up as he was in the colonial regional capital of Kaduna, an hour's drive away. My one or two encounters with him were friendly and encouraging.

The more important part of our link was certainly his shaping of a charismatic lecturer, Yusufu Bala Usman, the grandson of two emirs, one the famous Red Emir of Katsina who had supported Western education already a generation earlier. Thin and very tall, Bala was the graduate of an English university and was both a wonderful speaker (despite a cunningly used slight speech impediment) and an original and dynamic thinker who took Smith's ideas much further.[3] He was a radical nationalist but with a strong sympathy for Marxism – and he loved ideas. As I found out when I met him in London after leaving Nigeria, he had a discreet relationship with the American sociologist Norma Perchonok, also a friend who taught me a lot about the country. Norma, like Inez, was a large Jewish lady, in her case from a 'red diaper' family in Philadelphia. She would also elect to stay on and make her whole adult life in Northern Nigeria. Bala terrified most of my white colleagues, but Bob and I both had good relations with him and, as acting head, he would happily have had me stay on.

I should finally mention my closest Nigerian friend, George Kwanashie, who took me down to Lokoja – where the Benue, its greatest tributary, flows into the Niger – to visit home and cross the river in a canoe to court Clara, his future wife. I continued on to visit the hospitable Ade Obayemi, a Yoruba archaeologist with amazing language skills. I have

Figure 9.6: My colleague from Ahmadu Bello University, Yusufu Bala Usman, in Cape Town, 1997

said that Nigerian society seemed very closed, but with time, especially in my final year (1977–1978), it opened up and I had a positive relationship with the host of young men teaching in our department while doing their theses, no doubt under the redoubtable Abdullahi Smith. Clara Kwanashie eventually got a PhD herself, but in fact the maleness of our student body and faculty was still extremely obvious. There were few Nigerian women lecturing (apart from a small number from elsewhere in Africa) and not too many studying history, although Bala was in fact eager to encourage them in later years. All in all, my colleagues were both far more supportive and far more interesting than my previous experience of work.

I was generally the one left to teach about Europe, which I knew well, and so teaching influenced my politics very little, but it forced me to try to think about how to channel my knowledge in an African direction, as this was my audience. How much the students grasped as a result, I hate to think, but they worked hard and mostly ended up with second-class marks. There was almost a convention to make sure nobody got a first, and only the weakest few individuals wound up with thirds. The only suspense was over who was to get an upper, rather than a lower, second. But, generally speaking, that upper second encouraged holders to continue to graduate study, so it did have a real importance. Exam meetings, as we chewed the kola nuts passed around the table to keep us awake, went on for a long time. At least that was true in the final year when I was the last (Western) man standing.

On 13 February 1976, well into my first contract, General Murtala Mohammed, a Hausa from Kano who had replaced Gowon, the long-time post-civil war military head of state, was assassinated in a Lagos traffic jam on the way to work. This was part of a botched coup by some junior military Middle Belt people. For the bulk of Nigeria's tens of thousands of expatriates, this meant very little. One Nigerian military guy was for most purposes just like another. The professor of English, Bruce King, had made a long-standing plan for a Valentine's Day party at ABU that evening. I was not especially friendly with the Kings, so was not invited, but many I knew were. It isn't clear to me whether observant Nigerians were outraged at King's plan to carry on partying regardless of this major event in their political lives or whether there was a significant group looking for a moment to decisively dethrone Western influence and power at the university.

The party was broken up, a number of foreigners were temporarily arrested, and several, notably the Irish professor of political science, James O'Connell, were deported. The claim that he and others were intelligence agents for the British or American governments might have been true. Bob once told me that he was asked by some Americans if he would be interested in taking money for playing that role; nobody ever thought to ask me even though I had a few American friends in this very liberal-dominated politics department. Bala Usman was seen as the genius behind this stroke, and he was hated and feared by many of the expatriates I knew. It was certainly isolating to feel outside this new discourse of hostility in which the dwindling number of expatriates defended their practices as the essence of democracy and respectable university behaviour. I may have shared my quotidian life with them, but I was never comfortable with this way of understanding what we were doing.

My own views were in fact a mixture of politics and pragmatism. On the one hand, I had no desire to make my life in Nigeria and I did not imagine more than a very small percentage of other foreigners had that in mind either. I made a point of not attending governance meetings beyond the level of the department and took the point of view that it was very much up to the Nigerians what to make of the university. Clearly some aspects of its structure were imitative of the British model in ways that were not very appropriate. A large, overweeningly liberal crew of foreign political scientists full of the wisdom of US graduate schools didn't seem very appropriate to me either.

Apart from the pleasure I took in being able to live like a professional person rather than a student (I was to turn thirty-two in 1976), I was concerned to amass some savings from a minimum of two two-year contracts and to leave Nigeria no sooner than that with sufficient research material for a book. I was keenly aware that my thesis research had not led to my producing a book, which I assumed would be a requirement for a tenured job in the US. Most of my colleagues, inside and outside the department, looked successfully for ways to get out of Nigeria. By the autumn of 1977 there weren't many foreigners left in the humanities and social science parts of the university.

I carried on with my research, based mostly on car trips to Kaduna, where the Archives were (and as a resident of Nigeria, I did not have to make any excuses to get access to official papers of the past). I experienced some lonely times and suffered especially when, as happened very often, the electricity would go off for many hours. Looking through some papers from the time, I am reminded that this sense of isolation from the familiar was not psychologically good for me. It made me obsessive and distorted my judgement although not to the point that I realised it was time for me to move on. However, I actually had more space to get to know Nigerians and to be accepted by my colleagues as a familiar old hand. Here I saw the beginning of the end of the late-colonial university, with its priorities often marked out by progressive British academics of the left. The story of the University of Dar es Salaam, which shall come later, has been written up far more substantially. From Dar, in fact, came a former dean as our new post-Bob Gavin professor of history, after the exciting but straining time with Bala as acting head, in 1977. This was Arnold Temu, whose perhaps rather modest role as an historian with a Canadian doctorate must be overshadowed by his admirable critical assistance in developing a left intellectual culture in Dar es Salaam as an administrator in the late 1960s and the 1970s. He was an urbane and calming influence, making my final year in Nigeria pretty trouble-free work-wise.

This is probably a good place to discuss briefly my first book, *Capital and Labour on the Nigerian Tin Mines*. I didn't know how I could pursue South African history writing while living in Nigeria, so I felt I had to make a professional shift. The positive goal here was to try and write a very different kind of West African history. Modelling myself very consciously on *Chibaro*, Charles van Onselen's study of the early Rhodesian gold mining business with its powerful account of labour recruitment and work conditions, I attempted to insert political economy into that historiography and focus on an element of modern economic activity, albeit within a larger, essentially non-capitalist setting, in the colony as a whole. As pièce de résistance, I included the episode during World War II where forced labour was seriously abused but failed to lead to increased tin production. Here I finally achieved some success.[4] The book was taken up in the Longmans Ibadan History series against the advice of Nigeria's doyen of historians, Jacob Ajayi. I was the first non-Nigerian so selected, in good part thanks to the support of Michael Crowder, one of the key left-leaning post-war British historians of Africa, who, for my money, created its modern historiography in foundation. My book has many Google hits, I believe, but I think that is thanks to Nigerians who have bowdlerised it in a number of versions. But it failed to delight the mainstream West Africanists. They were partly right. I did virtually no fieldwork. By the time I wrote about them, the tin mines as a corporate venture had collapsed as a model of imperialism in the region and were a key exhibit in the later dominance of so-called artisanal mining. I did write a couple of shorter pieces that in effect changed focus towards this as the conclusion, but it took more contact with American Africanists a little later to figure out how to do this more effectively. In any case, the tin mines of the Jos Plateau were really the main reason I stayed on. And the book is a good study of political economy with a lot of insight into the society in which the mines developed as a work of history.

And, finally, there are sensual memories from the remarkable physical environment I inhabited: the leisurely visits of the men who laid out their wares in one's lounge during an afternoon and proceeded to bargain and eventually sell beautiful handicrafts, the lovely grapefruit trees in my garden, the travelling Yoruba theatre, the candle-lit charm of the night market in the old walled city of Zaria, the taste of purple onions so sweet they needed no cooking, the giant trays of carrots borne on Hausa heads when they were briefly in season, the build-up of heat and the mighty thunder showers of the rains once they began, the heat and the dust.

There was the extraordinary evening spent with Tony Humphries in Lagos at Fela Kuti's nightclub. The marijuana I smoked was so strong and satisfying that I fainted for once in my life. The nightclub people (Fela was actually not there) kindly revived me with advocaat in a back room, and Tony and I went off to sleep on the beach in Badagry, halfway to the Republic of Benin. It was a night to remember. There were also other explorations of Nigeria and farther afield in West Africa. I visited Ghana once after the Suttons moved there and drove both to Niger and to Cameroon.

And I cannot forbear to mention the creature in some ways dearer to me than almost all the people I have known: Ahmadu the black cat, who loved to sit on my shoulders or lie down beside me in bed on his back with the fan blowing when it was afternoon nap time, his paw in my hand. I brought him up and we were very fond of each other. I still think of the first time he purred in my company. I miss him, and he comes to mind very quickly when I think about Nigeria.

Figure 9.7: A successful tomato harvest in Zaria, 1978

Figure 9.8: My cat, Ahmadu

10 | An Intellectual and an African: Dar es Salaam and Harvard

Despite what had certainly become an attachment, leaving Nigeria was not much of a wrench; the discomforts involved in trying to lead a middle-class academic's life in this setting were too great. Those letters with job applications continued to get me absolutely nowhere, so I needed a plan. I managed to apply successfully to the American Social Science Research Foundation for a project that I had little intention of actually doing. This gave me a small income at the level of a graduate student for a year, which could be stretched. And a natural (by this time) if fateful decision was to choose to go to England, where I had passed a significant part of each summer vacation, particularly in 1977, as I shopped around for a place to make my headquarters. So in the middle of 1978 I left Nigeria again, never to return, with once again no job.

Here there are really two points to make. One was my distaste for the idea of going back to jobless America. I had little sense of post-Vietnam, Carter-era America and where it might be going and felt very out of touch, but there was nothing to attract me. Beside my range of friends in Britain and the largely British friends I made in Zaria, my way of expressing myself and living in a daily sense was in any case more and more English and less and less American.

The second was that, thanks to heeding Bob Shenton's wise instinct, I was finding my footing as what I am still today – a trained historian with a predilection for political economy, a strong interest in contemporary politics, and a sense of being at home in a milieu of Marxist and left scholarship, particularly focused on Africa and the Third World. And in England I

now regained my foothold in this community with some sense of belonging and attachment. I was very happy in this intellectual world in the late
1970s even if I could not for long push aside the realisation of how thin
my material foundation was for this life. During the two years that I stayed
in Britain on and off (1978–1980), I did finally get job interviews but the
market was tight, the competition more than respectable, and nothing in
the end came my way. Friendly as people generally were, I didn't have any
patrimonial or close connections that would put me to the fore. I was able
to stretch my little income through a short return to Africa, as I will relate
shortly.

England in the late 1970s was at a crossroads. The Labour Party in
power had a very thin majority under the leadership of James Callaghan.
His Conservative predecessor had presided over a major strike won by the
strikers. The unions were strong and successful despite the weak shape of
the economy. British capitalism had not grown very robustly after the end
of the war and it was now facing crisis conditions with particularly high
inflation and poor profit rates. London certainly contained a remarkable
service economy focused on tourism, the stock market and the presence of
wealthy foreigners, often from outside Europe. But Britain's old industries
were in bad shape, Harold Wilson's promised white heat of technology
was failing to promote any significant revival, and propping them up, with
Keynesian measures in place, wasn't working. What was to happen was a
swing towards the right, bringing the determined Margaret Thatcher to
power in 1979.

But for a time before that, it looked as though a left might be a serious
alternative. Much of the energy lay in a series of squabbling but not insub-
stantial Trotskyist sects, some with thousands of members and with varying relationships with Labour. They engaged a large range of intellectuals,
who could be found in every university, in many a subsidised bookshop,
in other organisations and, above all, in the trade unions. They conjoined
in academic institutions (notably the polytechnics) with the still vigorous
left intelligentsia of the 1930s and 1940s, often embodying a democratised
version of the old manners and habits, highly attractive to me, of the British
intelligentsia. It was a blessing to escape the starched shirt and dogmati-
cally liberal hegemony of US academic life. Like America, Britain also had
others mostly committed to racial justice or gender issues, but this Marxist

left tempered it with a very different and, to me, far more congenial balance. It was a kind of intellectual home that really pleased and excited me.

One striking feature was the commitment of so many to struggles in other parts of the world. South Africa occupied an outsize part of this. Some kind of South African story could be found weekly, indeed almost daily, in the quality newspapers. South African students mingled with South African exiles (both in Britain were largely white) and they were able to find means of supporting themselves and intellectual and academic work that was intended to be engaged. Shula Marks's seminars at SOAS continued and, in addition, Stan Trapido now had a postgraduate programme and a seminar series at Oxford too. There was a more mainstream centre at the University of York in the north, which would be the site of a politically important conference in the late 1980s. However, particularly to my taste was yet another seminar series set up at the University of Warwick with the intention of highlighting labour organisation (and thus reflecting labour insurgency and its supporters in South Africa itself) by Martin Legassick, who had now abandoned history for sociology. It's hard not to recall getting a lift from Martin in a car, otherwise disorderly, lumbered with various editions of Marx as well as Militant literature. Militant was a Trotskyist group that worked within Labour and eventually sponsored a few members of parliament, just as the South African Communist Party (SACP) worked within the ANC. Martin disliked the SACP and he attracted a host of independent-minded individuals who formed a distinct community with whom I redeployed my own interest in South Africa. His group called themselves the Marxist Workers' Tendency of the ANC. This mixture of politics and social science captured my imagination. The students and associates who came to seminars at Warwick were a highly intelligent, mostly very dedicated and also very congenial group of South Africans, some of whom I would continue to know after I came to live in their country.

Warwick also then lived in the shadow of the great social historian and independent (and ex-Communist) leftist, Edward Thompson. Thompson was able to manage without a job and had given up his teaching career, but the Centre for the Study of Social History carried on. This was the centre that I chose as my base in England under its courtly head, Royden Harrison. I was an outsider in respect of knowledge of English social and labour history, but some of the work being done inspired me. I was privileged enough at least twice to hear talks by Thompson, one in Oxford and one in Coventry. Thompson's sense of the English political crisis was illuminating despite the lack of light due to a power strike, and his book *Writing by Candlelight* was important to me. So was the work he did in interpreting material liberated from university files in a sit-in, published as *Warwick University Ltd*, which examined the success (and consequences) of the university in servicing the private sector, notably the brewing trade.[1] I retained, and perhaps still retain, a somewhat old-fashioned idea about what ought to motivate university life which harmonises pretty well with older radical beliefs. Among the people I met in this context was a sociologist, Bob Fine, who took the common left interest in South Africa and who convinced me of the charms of his own 'entryist' Trotskyist group within Labour, which was associated with a journal called *Socialist Organiser*. He had a strong libertarian side to his thinking as well as some North American experience and became a close friend. I learnt a lot from him, especially in clarifying a political vision of my own.

Coventry's city centre had been destroyed in World War II by German bombing and it had little to attract custom. The university lay on the outskirts next to open fields and farms in the outlying direction. So I knew the city very little. Instead I lived, as did many university people, in the old spa town of Leamington. Leamington had become a mill town with a distinct community of Indian Sikh immigrants, but around the old spa centre lay streets lined with mid-Victorian buildings and cheap rents, in one of which I inhabited a small apartment. There was even a Regency crescent where Thompson had lived in style. A bus from the centre passed near to the university but it was neither frequent nor fast. Equally slow, not very reliable though convenient enough was the train line south through Oxford to London, two hours away. Cheap housing attracted alternative people of all sorts, and Leamington did have a pleasant high street full of life on a Saturday. I remember looking with some yearning at the windows of estate agents and dreaming about a more comfortable life as an ensconced radical lecturer, but in fact I had pretty much the existence of a foreign graduate student at most. This was fine at first but less and less so as time passed by.

As I have already mentioned, during my Leamington phase I had not just a bunch of new friends, some of whom would carry through to my life in South Africa in future, but I was able to establish connections that gave me a kind of presence in an intellectual world I felt fitted me well. Down the road was my fast friend Gavin Williams of St Peter's College, Oxford. Gavin had been a Rhodes Scholar from Durban, who went to Oxford and returned there as an academic. He could be said to combine Marxist and liberal ideas, with Weber as his main intellectual prop, but he was very open-minded. Gavin's research work had been on Nigeria, and his combination of knowledge of and interest in both his country of birth and Nigeria, apart from his natural generosity and good spirits, made him at once an important and influential friend.

Gavin was one of the founder-members of the *Review of African Political Economy* collective, RAPE, which would soon become ROAPE, and he shared my sense of critique of mainstream analyses of African society and politics. ROAPE also had a remarkably committed bibliographer in Chris Allen of the University of Edinburgh, who perhaps remembered me from 1969 when he worked under Thomas Hodgkin at Oxford and participated in seminars which I attended. Chris tried to put me forward for a job that I never got in Edinburgh, but he needs to be mentioned because of his influence with the publishing house of Macmillan. Macmillan asked me to propose a book of interpretation of African history. I had no idea if I would ever have a chance to teach my ideas about African history but I had acquired quite a few in my Nigerian career. I had the knowledge of two very different countries and would soon acquire a third interest this way, and I was eager to have a try. It was an attempt to put into practice those ideas that had been with me since reading Hobsbawm: writing an African history that was neither a sentimental and potentially patronising attempt to identify with racialised victims nor a colonial apologia, but rather a synthesis that integrated the economic, the political and the cultural while making sure that political economy was always at the heart of historical analysis. I read voluminously for this work and, indeed, later for future editions, and that included work by scholars from outside the Anglosphere and by Africans when possible. I tried to bring out some new ideas. For example, it seemed to me that in the two generations before imperialist conquest, a variety of powerful militarised African states had been proceeding to carve up much of the continent themselves. Trekking Boers in South Africa were one of these forces. Few, if any, of these states, which mostly picked up European weaponry, had many scruples about slaving. Some could certainly be seen as moving forward in terms of material development.

When I wrote *The Making of Contemporary Africa*, I tried hard to find a balance between the oppressive side of imperialism, emphasised in my first book, and the reality that imperialism was related to globalisation, to bringing Africans new opportunities and new socio-cultural forms speeding up innovation. John Flint, an Englishman who taught African history at Dalhousie University in Canada, wrote an interesting review in which he noted quite correctly that I used Marxist terms but was not interested primarily in writing a denunciation of the West or imperialism. Imperialism happens, and, in an industrial era, it did take a form that fitted aspects of capitalism and that suited its drive for accumulation. In the very much later third edition, I used the last chapter to try to describe briefly changes that African society has encompassed since the end of colonialism and to differentiate between increasingly different outcomes in various states.

Before I left England, I received an advance and started to write this book, which is certainly the one by which I am best known. Working on it began to fill my time in Leamington. Initially in 1978 I had decided not to opt for the Centre of West African Studies in Birmingham as a place to write; that was a fateful choice. While I saw through my Nigerian research and Longmans put out my tin mining book shortly after I left England, I never really wrote again directly about West Africa. I was more and more interested in resuming South African work, but this did not yet seem practicable.

Thanks to Martin Legassick, I believe, there was an important interlude in my Warwick years, lasting only for an extended term but deserving of some attention itself. There was a deal between the British government and the University of Dar es Salaam in Tanzania which paid for academics based in Britain to go out for short teaching stints. I got included in this bunch as did Martin's student David Hemson, a banned South African writing a long and important thesis on the history of Durban dock workers. As a result, in the second half of 1979, it was back to Africa for me.

Tanzania was a considerable contrast to Nigeria. The city of Dar es Salaam had a far larger Indian (especially) and white population compared with any equivalent in Nigeria. At the same time, Tanzania was a poor country. The president, Julius Nyerere, had pursued a policy of socialist self-reliance that ironically attracted massive foreign aid, notably from Scandinavia, and an independent, often quite shrewd foreign policy. Neutrality in the Cold War led to Tanzania being very attractive to donors. By 1979 contradictions in the system Nyerere tried to initiate were beginning to widen and cause ever-deeper problems. Tanzania had very limited mineral resources as far as was then known. It depended on a bouquet of agricultural exports, and the international prices for all of them – cashew nuts, coffee, cotton and so on – were becoming poorer and poorer. Nyerere bought out the small white settler community and discouraged private accumulation either by the Indian merchant class or by enterprising Africans, for instance those dominating the cooperatives. Autonomous civil society, whether in the form of those cooperatives or militant trade unions, was discouraged to the point of repression. The state consisted of a new class of black bureaucrats who were not able to orchestrate an accumulation process that could take the country forwards economically. Thus conditions were degenerating constantly, leading for instance to massive shortages.

The university was located on a beautiful campus well outside the town. Here it was comparable to the situation I knew in Zaria. It was much smaller than ABU but it absorbed at peak no less than half the entire education budget of the Tanzanian government. A clash with students over their conditions of living led to the state imposing its will on the university. It was generally impossible to gain admission without having a career and being nominated by the ruling party first. Teaching was pleasant enough; I remember having only six perfectly competent if unexciting students.

But during the 1970s the university had also become a hotbed of radical activity. It not only hosted many of those formulating radical ideas about African society; it was a community that generated such ideas. Many of these stars, such as Lionel Cliffe, Walter Rodney, Mahmood Mamdani and John Saul, had moved on by 1979. It became clear that their ideas were too independent for the ruling party and for Nyerere, who favoured a more nationalist line. A Ugandan political scientist, Dan Nabudere, more puffed by hot air and empty rhetoric than substance, excoriated the Marxists and put forward what was really a crude nationalist perspective. However, he too had moved on a little before my time. Among the Tanzanians who were influenced by and had felt attracted to Marxist ideas were the former dean, Arnold Temu, who had recently been hired by Zaria, and Bonaventure Swai, my department head. Swai was a far less aggressive figure than Bala Usman and was always a bit drunk on books and ideas. He did some interesting theoretical, semi-polemical writing that related well to my own ideas about melding development and historical studies. He told me that his wife had warned him that she would leave him if he did not emerge out of his piles of books. He was certainly a positive element in creating a pleasant and quite stimulating atmosphere.

When I think of the department, I can't but mention Sid Lemelle, a UCLA history product, who wrote about mining in colonial Tanganyika. Sid was intended by the priests, who educated him as a schoolboy, to become Los Angeles' first black dentist. However, an English professor in the commuter college he attended after the military (where he did practise some dentistry) converted him to a fascination with history. At UCLA he found in Ned Alpers one of the few American historians of Africa with an interest in left ideas and a bent for economic history. Through Sid, I began to get to know a minority community of black radicals in America attracted to Marxist theory. I used to nap in the heat at his house after I lectured. We had some good times together where we shared ideas and hung out with others as well.

The left intellectual community was very congenial to me. I look back on Dar as a very nice time, but I also was sobered by this experience. I had admired in a general way so much of the Nyerere line and the idea of an Africanised socialist project. But I came to see with my own eyes that this extremely poor country had to find a way, through its majority African population or its racial minorities, through potential capitalist businesses or an efficient developmental state, to accumulate skills, infrastructure and wealth. In the world as it was constituted, articulating one's ideas was definitely not enough. Without a road to accumulation, this country could go nowhere. I wrote a short piece that tried to make this point, which was published in time in *African Affairs*. It is a great pity that today Tanzania has found various new sources of wealth but there is little effort to keep some of the ideals of the past so as to channel them in ways that build a better life for people systematically. At least the traditions of the ruling party, the Chama Cha Mapinduzi, have done a good job in holding the country together without the typical competitive ethnic patronage politics that spoil everything in so much of Africa.

I also became a good friend of Dave Hemson (with whom I went on a memorable weekend excursion to Zanzibar, then just opening up to tourists after years of North Korea-like isolation). Through him, I met the first of the new generation of South African radical sociology students at the University of Sussex. This was Dan O'Meara, who was in the process of moving to Maputo and who wrote so effectively about economic power in South Africa and the Afrikaner political elite. The other members of the 'gang of four' I would meet in South Africa: Dave Kaplan in Cape Town, Mike Morris in Durban, and Rob Davies, the current minister of trade and industry, after his return from exile.

Dave was not only in Tanzania to commune with Dan. The ANC exiles had an important base in the country and Dave, like Martin Legassick, was connected to the Marxist Workers' Tendency in the ANC. This was, to put it mildly, not generated by the leadership. Indeed, the exile leaders felt threatened by the emergence of ideas created by the new insurgent trade union movement in the country and the untamed new generation of township-bred youths who were not yet politically committed to a party and were clearly of first-rate importance. Catching them if they fled across the border and turning them into liberation movement cadres was a top priority for the ANC. The Marxist Workers' Tendency was a problem in its out-and-out support for the independent unions, its raising of issues more convenient to leave undiscussed, and its hostility to the South African Communist Party. At the same time, it was hardly a flag to wave that could attract liberal international supporters of the growing anti-apartheid movement.

This phase when I was in Dar was their moment of truth: Joe Slovo personally called on Hemson to reprimand him and expel him from the party. Perhaps I would have been charmed by Joe myself; Dan loved him dearly. But by chance I never met him. He called on me once in the course of one of my famous afternoon naps and failed to rouse me, so that was it. My distaste for the inability of the supposed broad church of the ANC to tolerate a bunch of Trotskyites with some very good ideas, as opposed to the acceptable common prejudices of potentially recruitable black South Africans, led to a distancing that confirmed what I had already gathered from the South African friends I trusted and relied on. To this was added my sense, from what I could pick up, that Umkhonto we Sizwe, the armed wing of the party, was not a serious guerrilla army in the making. I have never been an enemy of the ANC, which incidentally has done much good in power, but I could also never see myself as an uncritical friend, let alone a 'cadre'.

There was not much to encourage an enthusiastic leftist about Tanzania in 1979 any longer. However, the exchange programme did attract a varied and impressive group of academics on a short-term stay like me. This made for a very congenial and stimulating time. We all stayed at the slightly woebegone Hotel Silver Sands on the ocean, run for this purpose by the university. This was a relic from the days when whites lived in some numbers in Tanganyika and there was a small tourist economy in operation. Very often I would go out into the sea in the afternoon with goggles and look at the amazing life around a big rock not very far out when the tide was in. Tanzanians were much friendlier to outsiders than Nigerians had been, and there was no reason to envy visitors like me for holding down posts that they craved for themselves. With some of them I shared political ideas and I very much enjoyed speaking some Kiswahili successfully (while I had never learnt more than the basic elements of Hausa). In general, I have fond memories of the country and it has been a pleasure to return in post-apartheid years on different errands, renewing after many years a number of congenial acquaintances.

Instead of returning directly to Leamington Spa, I was sufficiently positive about life to want to see in the new year in India. Here I spent almost a month travelling at a time when there were Indrail passes at little expense and accommodation and food were also very cheap. The plane had some technical problem and so I spent a day or two in the then remote and beautiful Seychelles en route (the site of a fairly left-wing government that has had some long-term positive impacts). At this stage, Indian democracy, so often put forward as a kind of model for the world outside the West, had been shaken by the experience of Indira Gandhi's State of Emergency. But this had come to an end in the 1977 election and the left was on the rise in various parts of the country. You could see some sign of union militancy on the rail network, which still included steam trains.

This was a much-longed-for travel destination and it gave me a sense of the difference between India and Africa. I remember an Indian colleague based in Canada who made what I thought was a fascinating comparison. In Tanzania (he was a scientist) he had access apparently to some expensive and impressive equipment. But this stuff simply came as a gift through the aid networks; when something failed to work, it was simply abandoned. Nobody knew how, or cared enough, to repair it and it would sit gathering dust. In India, the keystone projects were donated by Russia. These were simply turned over to Indian recipients. They certainly had faults and were far from perfect, but Indians had the expertise and the commitment to fix and apply them in order to build the economy. I have made this comparison in a way in a *Transformation* article (2004) with South Africa. Once upon a time, South Africa sold machinery to India in exchange for raw materials. Now it is quite the other way around. This was how I saw in the year 1980, the new decade in fact.

It was, of course, very sobering to return to Margaret Thatcher's England. It was clear that a job at an English university or polytechnic would be a huge ask in this new environment. So what was there to do? I could perhaps return to Nigeria or find something else in Africa but, as I have already said, by this stage I was longing for a secure life in the West and was now past the middle of my thirties.

Instead an intervention took me by surprise. Fred Cooper had found a job for me at Harvard University, where he was temporarily situated. The senior Africanist, indeed the first-ever Nigerian to get a history PhD, was Kenneth O. Dike. An Igbo, Dike had gone into exile as a result of the Biafran War but he was getting old and wanted to return to his homeland.[2] When I flew over to Boston to see about the job, all he wanted to know was whether I had Nigerian experience and would be writing about Nigeria, a point on which I could certainly reassure him. So he left and I organised my return, my last return to my own native country on a one-year contract that eventually swelled into three years. I looked forward to the companionship of Fred. I also knew Boston a little, had a few friends that I could visit such as Hildy Armour and Larry Finison from my Kirkland days, and found it an atmospheric and attractive city with a rich cultural life. But after my years among British Trotskyists accustomed to social democratic benefits, the politics of Tanzania and even India or Albert René's Seychelles, I was quite unprepared for the conservative turn that had taken hold in the US. Not long after I arrived, the arch-villain of the Berkeley Free Speech Movement and former governor of California, the dreadful Ronald Reagan, was elected president. This was the national mood when I came back to live in America for over three years.

Harvard University was probably not very different from Yale. But Harvard was also particularly associated with the US government as opposed to the Stock Exchange and the corporate world. The students I had were rarely shy of ambition. It had a great urban location, the Widener was a great library, and there were some nice side-features. For instance, I learned to row a scull on the Charles. I took up yoga for a while and, with the help of yoga, weaned myself off cigarettes.

The one obvious continuity with my existence in Britain was my very small salary and continued existence not too far from the poverty line. Essentially the job I had was at a level usually given to a clever postgraduate student who had somehow not found a job in the first year out, the sort of thing that might deservedly have been offered to me a decade earlier. My relationship was thus very different from that at graduate school at Yale. The History Department had a building all to itself near the art gallery and

Figure 10.1: In Boston, 1982

the far corner of Harvard Yard, in front of which was the bicycle rack I used. The small community of untenured assistant professors and lecturers, as I was labelled, had offices together in the basement. The others had appointments to cover several years whereas I had simply a year's contract. Fred left Harvard after the first two years, so there was a vacuum in African history which enabled me to stay three years in all.

I enjoyed my teaching at Harvard very much. Some of the students were very bright indeed and a pleasure to know. This was the beginning of the era when teachers got rated by students, and I had very high ratings – but also very small enrolments in a college where history was in fact the most popular undergraduate major, rife as the place was with future lawyers and would-be Washington lobbyists and power brokers. I continued as well to feel at times like a referee between fairly mutually hostile white and black students, although I had friends on both sides.

A positive side of my job, apart from the students, lay in the light teaching load, which enabled me to get on with writing. The Nigerian tin mine book came out and I finished *The Making of Contemporary Africa* in time to see it in a New York bookstore before I left America in mid-1984. My interest in labour issues was rewarded by an invitation by Allen Isaacman, the University of Minnesota historian, to produce one of the series of long papers for the US Social Science Research Council (SSRC) on labour and labour history. Allen was one of the very few US specialists on Africa whose interests broadly connected with my own. This paper has more Google hits than any other article I have written (albeit fewer than any of my books) and I was persuaded to expand it into a third book, which I began to write before my departure.

I had an amiable enough relationship with the very varied array of junior professors, but none was remotely close to my interests or experience. Indeed, I was quite aware of the fact that my students, including the black ones, came from more impressive class backgrounds in US terms than I did.

However, this was an era when I did collect friends from the left community and notably from individuals interested in Africa. I joined a radical history reading group and I regularly crossed the Charles River on my bicycle to go to African studies seminars at Boston University half an hour or less away. My friends of the time included, apart from passing individuals, A.M. Babu, the well-known Zanzibari intellectual and exile; Hussein Bulhan, a Somali friend who was a politicised psychiatrist; Jordan Gebre-Medhin, an Eritrean political scientist (and close neighbour); and Mark Kaplan, a South African/Zimbabwean exile enrolled in MIT's famous film course. I do need to mention the seminar organiser, Bill Hansen.[3] Bill had picked up the seminar habit in England, as it is hardly a US university practice normally, and put time and energy into this successful initiative. He had a remarkable history in the civil rights movement, having become the Student Nonviolent Coordinating Committee (SNCC) head organiser for the state of Arkansas in the early 1960s, and he is enshrined in quite a few of the histories written on the movement. Bill's affection for black nationalism was certainly greater than mine. He and his German wife, Gitte, were happy for lots of company, and I would normally spend a weekend evening with them in Watertown, cycling back home to Cambridgeport late at night. Bill certainly tried, sometimes with success, to give the seminars a cast that interested me. However, I have also to record my gratitude that I was permitted to participate in the discussions of a group of women specialists in Africa, notably Jane Guyer, Sara Berry, Sharon Stichter, Jane Parpart, Jean Hay, Pauline Peters and Jeanne Henn. They had interesting and new things to say about African society that were tied into economic concerns but foregrounded family relationships and the standpoint of women as economic actors and household members. I hope my work sense profited from this dimension, which was a minor revolution at the time in African studies, one that did fit American predilections. It also reflected one positive development, the variety of colleges and universities that seemed to have materialised in every neighbourhood of Boston and, in this case, the possibility of specialists crossing the institutional lines to come together, which is not very usual.

Boston is notoriously not a friendly town, but its roots are really old. Getting a sense of its relationship with the sea, including its great seafood, and its distinctive communities, beyond the education and health sectors, that brought together an international and national elite was not without fascination. But I remember feeling if I pushed my bike all the way to the waterfront that it was a comfort to be only half an hour away on two wheels from water on the other side of which was no longer America. I benefited from a small assortment of old friends who had come to settle there, such as Tom Leighton, who left New York in 1983 for his boyhood home city. However, at that very time my job came to an end without any alternative.

Being a lecturer in history at Harvard, as I was designated, was, to my shock, in no way a fine reintroduction to the US job market. Absolutely nothing came my way: no interviews, no anything. In the first year I felt good about trying out a new life with the tools I had acquired. In the mid-1980s, despite my success on the publication front and despite quite a few pleasures and interesting experiences and new friendships, my precarious existence led me to a sense of despair. I really did not know which way to turn and I no longer knew what I could possibly do to improve my chances of survival.

One positive experience that began by chance would finally open a door for me. Chris Saunders, once a contemporary of mine and Oxford graduate student whom I enjoyed knowing in Cape Town, was now a rising academic at the university in that city where he had himself initially studied. To some degree, we remained in contact. Chris had some involvement with the Students' Visiting Lecturers Trust Fund that allowed the Student Representative Council to bring an interesting foreigner to the University of Cape Town (UCT) as an academic visitor. At UCT the liberal identity and the need to feel accepted in the Anglo-American academic establishment world were imperative, and this was the kind of gesture that the government allowed and that was easy to put into practice. For 1982, the choice was an American, the late Leroy Vail, whom Harvard would eventually hire as their permanent historian of Africa. Fairly late in the day, Leroy turned UCT down. Chris proposed my name that spring – I was getting to be well-enough known at the time – and I was asked to come to Cape Town for the summer, more than twelve years after I finished my PhD research there. I accepted, of course, with alacrity. This visit was to change my life again.

Cape Town and South Africa had changed dramatically in the twelve years that I had been gone. Once one had talked about South Africa's businesses having an untroubled ride, with growth assured and inevitably linked to an impoverished black labour force. Now growth was poor and South Africa in 1982 was nearing the end of the good times. The rand was now worth half a US dollar instead of being more than a dollar in value, although it was to start shrinking much further. The economy was also under strain from the growing impact of sanctions and disinvestment.

Moreover, the country was, to put it mildly, no longer at peace. There was an active so-called border war and massive amounts were spent every year on defence requirements. The townships were periodically uneasy after the major explosion of 1976. On the one hand, this engendered a growing militarisation and very unhealthy signs of a security state somewhat out of control. Captured guerrillas were either turned by their gaolers or killed. Hit squads also killed troublemakers, including a number of white intellectuals suspected of ANC links. On the other hand, byzantine constitutional changes were in the offing that would bring people of colour into the system. The ties meant to make sure that they remained within defined limits were not so easy to keep fastened entirely. Behind this lay the growing view among high state officials, not to speak of the business community, that these problems would never go away under the banner of apartheid or even under a government that excluded the African majority. The time of negotiations, secret negotiations, was near at hand.

This was a truly fascinating scenario, albeit one where levels of violence were rising. The universities run for English-speaking whites were in any case almost entirely unsympathetic to the government; they looked to Big Brother in perhaps America or certainly Britain for material and moral guidance. Rhodes Scholarships and links to Oxford and to Chatham House were critical, even though the growth in the student body of these universities lay more and more in the professional subjects that either guaranteed a comfortable life or made for an easy exit to somewhere safe and stable in the Anglosphere. White men were 'conscientised', to use the term of that time, through the imposition of universal conscription; only a minor issue in 1969, it now had much the same impact as Vietnam War-era conscription in America.[4] Overwhelmingly white, the universities could, however, invite speakers for particular occasions as they liked, and hire faculty as they liked, and they attracted students of colour in small numbers who qualified by majoring in subjects taught only in white institutions. Loopholes on the racial frontier were growing and racial intermarriage was soon to become legal again. In my case, there were two additional pluses. The intellectual strength of the independent left in Britain and the growing interest in the ANC and its Communist ally made for a warm welcome to a foreign comrade, as I was made to feel. There was equally a fascination with doings elsewhere in Africa, notably in Zimbabwe, which South

Africans could easily visit, and Tanzania with its political track record. My knowledge of this world was also something that opened doors.

Chris Saunders's History Department, while I made some friends in it, was basically a staunchly liberal affair. However, there was also a separate Economic History Department where radical activists flourished. Here I met Dave Kaplan, one of the notorious 'gang of four'; Alan Hirsch, eventually to become a speechwriter for Nelson Mandela and economic policy adviser to Thabo Mbeki; and the head of the show, Ian Phimister, a Rhodesian escaping military duties there – all very bright, all very interested in a host of extracurricular, politically tinged activities, and all extremely sociable. And there were others from other departments and they led on to activists from the various professions. A sense of community, which emerged out of the isolation of this growing network from mainstream white (or, for that matter, black) society, was manifest and welcoming. It was an incomparably more attractive intellectual setting for me than Harvard.

By the end of my weeks in Cape Town (and I also visited Johannesburg and, for the first time, my future home of Durban), I timidly asked whether it was an outrageous idea for me to think of looking for a job in South Africa. I was certainly moved also by being in a setting where there were no unemployed PhDs and it was quite reasonable to aspire to a comfortable life if one had a university position. The attraction of beautiful scenery and a life without a hard Northern winter didn't lack for appeal either.

Of course, South Africa appeared as well to be a really risky place. I would reluctantly have taken an American job if anyone had offered me one in 1982–1984, so my plan of entering the job market there was essentially a fall-back. However, it seemed like a much better bet than returning to ABU or some equivalent even if I could find a position elsewhere in Africa. My instinct was that the system could not endure in its old form but also that the liberation movements had little prospect of actually seizing power. There would be a stalemate. Eventually things would open up more and some kind of compromise could ensue. Here, of course, I prophesied correctly.

It was already true that I could essentially teach and write as I liked in South Africa, from what I could see from my UCT experience. If teaching and writing without any grandstanding was where I could make a contribution, this was good enough. I was willing to brave the academic boycott that would be increasingly imposed, though also selectively violated, in order to make a life for myself. I had no intention in any event of becoming an underground agent of the ANC or of any competing liberation group.

I also believed that I could work at a South African university in such a way as to be in touch with and helpful to what was then called the independent union movement. It was in fact all the way back in 1969 that the Durban dockers first went on strike. This was the first small blow in a line of development that, with fits and starts, gained strength through the 1970s. A new trade union movement was born, and it captured the energies of white students who did not want to emigrate and who were not welcome in student organisations, thanks to Black Consciousness and the approach of its martyred leader Steve Biko, who advocated black separatism as an organising strategy. White students became the intellectuals and the organisers of the new trade unions, which Black Consciousness almost entirely ignored. One hallmark was that the influence of these activists was matched by their promotion of workplace autonomy and worker voice in which the empowerment of the shop stewards was administratively key.

What was largely (but, to be fair, not entirely) missing was the politicos, who would have liked to lasso the unions in the interests of the underground and the ANC. The ANC had previously sponsored the now exiled South African Congress of Trade Unions, which organised among blacks almost exclusively and, once illegal, tried to push the 1950s unions into focusing on ANC commitments, particularly into sustaining an underground armed struggle. The 'independent' unions were, in varying degrees, quite hostile to this approach and avoided any open political affiliation. This in turn made it possible for them to function legally despite enormous state disapproval and, at times, persecution. The question whether they should go for registration with the state and whether they were prepared to declare themselves consequently only for blacks by definition was a hot one when I arrived. While the exiled ANC was very hostile to this independence at first, the growing strength of the independents and their ability to mount international solidarity campaigns made it increasingly problematic for them to be simply ignored or pushed aside. Eventually, these two forces would come together.

In the meantime, I was very delighted to meet and make friends with young people who had plunged into a politics that resonated with my own beliefs. Of course, Martin Legassick had a great interest in these unions too and many contacts with them, which served me in good stead. The Warwick past gave me important contacts in this direction. The union links to economic history were particularly important, and these were economic historians who were first and foremost labour historians. A labour history stressing social issues and organisation as well as the oppression of black workers was rapidly emerging. The unions, a subject of almost no interest in African studies circles in the US, were also a major pole of attraction for me.[5]

The academic year 1982–1983, as I imagined from the start, was to be the last one in which I had employment at Harvard. Fred had moved on to the University of Michigan and I was now something between angry and depressed when I contemplated my situation. This difficult mood persisted for a yet longer period until I finally came to South Africa to live, in the Northern spring of 1984. As for my work, this was the period when I wrote *The African Worker*, certainly very influenced by the ties I had forged with the South African trade union world, following the SSRC long paper.

The chief professional adventure here lay in a misfire. I returned to Cape Town once again when my work ran out in Cambridge, Massachusetts, in 1983 and, encouraged by new friends in Durban, applied for a professorship there. I don't know what was at stake, but in fact an American political scientist was appointed ahead of me in African Studies. This was a terrible blow at the time. However, Ian Phimister contacted Charles van Onselen, whom I knew a little and who was in fact in charge of the African Studies Institute at the University of the Witwatersrand in Johannesburg, and Charles was able to accommodate me with a three-year research position at the Institute. So I returned to America with the most secure job offer in the thirteen years in which I had been trying for one. However, there now had to be a wait for a visa to return to South Africa and take the job. Given the suspicious nature of the South African state at the time, this not only took some time to organise, but it also was not a sure thing. During these winter months in Cambridge, I earned nothing and, indeed, also had the anxiety that my landlord wanted access to my Magazine Street apartment and understandably wanted me out.

I had revealed my adventurous side from Dar es Salaam in buying a ticket to Bombay and spending a month touring India without a job and with very little money. This time a plan arose with Tom Leighton and a friend of his to go for a vacation, partly spent with them and partly on my own, in Mexico. On the eve of this trip, miraculously the visa came. At this point it was by most ideas spring, but the cold was still there and a late storm dumped snow on Massachusetts. Somehow it seemed imperative to carry out the Mexican plan. I can remember well trudging through the snow on Magazine Street to catch the subway to the airport. In the end, via Miami, we landed in the balmy sunshine in Mexico City. I was very taken with Mexico, my first extended visit to Latin America, so this was really a first prelude to a new life for me. The next flight was to Chicago, where I collected a variety of things I would need in the coming weeks in Johannesburg.

Here what I remember was driving to O'Hare Airport on that errand. The reason the trip was memorable was that my father asked me if he could come along and we had lunch along the way. This was a nice gesture of reconciliation, unprecedented as it was, and it somehow fitted my mood of reaching a kind of end to my American life. It was a counterweight to telephoning my mother after I had failed to get the job in Durban: she obviously assumed right at the start that I would fail, as I always did (or perhaps was pleased, as it might mean I would come back to America for good). This was the end of my having much feeling for her except within narrow limits. The last time we ever went to a concert together, we listened to Górecki's moving and beautiful Third Symphony at a Northwestern University venue. This was a context where I could relate to her, and a good memory of her from her last years. I certainly feel guilty or anxious at times that I had so little to offer her and that she had so little to offer me as an adult. In truth I left America without a moment of regret or sorrow and have never had any desire to return. My dislike for the place never disappeared. Indeed, it reached a climax in 2016 when Americans actually elected the bigot Donald Trump as president, although in policy terms his opponent Hillary Clinton pleased me almost as little. The actual move to Johannesburg was made easier by the fact that, apart from books, I had accumulated so few possessions thus far. It really was the start of a new life.

11 | South Africa, My Home

In the end I stayed well under a year at the African Studies Institute (ASI) in Johannesburg. After several months, the geography lecturer Alan Mabin brought me together with two of his friends from Durban, geographer Jeff McCarthy and planner Mike Sutcliffe, both holders of doctorates from Ohio State University. Another Durban option had emerged and they succeeded in talking me into applying. And this time, the job, for a newly created professorship of economic history, was offered to me. I hesitated out of gratitude to Charles van Onselen, who was understandably annoyed at my leaving, but the idea of a permanent job, as South Africans refer to this kind of situation, and an end to those long years of uncertainty – and, after all, I now had turned forty – was too good to refuse. What I did see in Durban was the warm sea, the luxuriant vegetation and the mild winter climate. Johannesburg winter nights are cold and, after my wait in Boston, my body felt that it was experiencing a whole year of winter weather, so Durban was even more seductive. I also liked Jeff, Mike, and particularly Dan North-Coombes and his new partner, Jo Beall. Dan was a lecturer in economic history, a remarkable, erudite and dedicated Mauritian from a family that settled in South Africa via Rhodesia, a route that followed the sugar cane industry trail. Dan had a somewhat different take on race from what a South African would but, a rather late convert, he had become both an enemy of racism and a very well-read Marxist thinker; he was then organising his PhD research after having already produced an MA in economic history at the University of Cape Town (UCT). It all seemed too good to pass up. As a result I gave up my little flat on Sharp Street in Bellevue, Johannesburg, and began what would be my life in the city of Durban.

Figure 11.1: In Johannesburg, 1984

I should, however, comment on my days in Johannesburg where I met many people, some of whom have remained my friends over decades. Charles had a poor relationship with Eddie Webster, the leading light in Sociology, for reasons I can't really discern even now. Eddie has played a remarkable part in connecting his department to the renewed labour movement; indeed, its links continue to this day. Friendship with Eddie meant that I got called into service to 'monitor' the Vaal Rising of mid-1984, a protest that began with resentment at the high service charges being imposed for the introduction of better amenities in a big township south of Johannesburg. This marked a new wave, bigger than ever, of resistance, quite violent and with its heart in the townships – 'the youth' – rather than the trade unions. I realised from this experience in particular that the reform impetus from the state was not going to work, whether it petered out or intensified, and that the South African political crisis had considerable space to run. The first State of Emergency was declared in 1985, but it struck me that reform was going to be retained, if not accelerated, and that further change, however it came, was certain. This reinforced my sense that my new life was not being built on too shaky a basis.

While I worked at the ASI, I was mostly busy finishing *The African Worker* for Cambridge University Press. However, I also began to tinker with the industrial and economic themes to which I have largely stuck ever since. The ASI job contained within it a requirement to teach one final-year history course, which I was happy to do. This was a different kind of group from what I had experienced before in either Africa or America. At the top end of the scale, Matt Chaskalson, later to be a professor of law and son of a future chief justice, paid me the compliment of attending my lectures. The best student, who himself later became a professor of history, was Clive Glaser, and yet a third Jewish student, Laura Menachemson, also stood out. Then there was a gap. Only a few students, white males aiming at a further law degree plus a few Indian young men who had been denigrated by the more conservative department members, had the middling grades you would assume were the norm. The majority were very mediocre indeed, able to grasp only the basics, if that, of what I was saying and what they should have been reading. Many came from rising working-class immigrant families; the better students would have been in medicine or engineering or some such discipline. But attending to this majority was not really expected of me, just as it could be presumed that the bright few were anti-apartheid stalwarts already, perhaps very active ones. I had also done some teaching at Honours level (the year required after the three-year first degree) at UCT. That had been an outstanding group. It included Ciraj Rassool and Les Bank, both future academics and authors. Ciraj had been formed politically by the Unity Movement, a grouping with support largely among Coloured intellectuals and largely in the Cape. The Unity Movement was dying out organisationally but had a strong hold on intellectuals, and its understanding of the nature of South Africa and in particular the 'national question' – race – deserved that hold. Unfortunately it had developed a sect-like character and had little mass appeal. I mention this because it was actually Ciraj I asked when seeking the opinion of someone who was not white (the Rassools are Indian) about my coming to an academic job in South Africa. His thumbs-up was important to my decision. This marvellous UCT class, however, did not give a real indication of what teaching in South Africa would be like, though the days at Wits were a good prelude.

As my fortieth year came to an end, I left the new friends in Johannesburg and drove down to Durban and the flat assigned to me in Shepstone Building. Whatever the flaws in the institution, my gratitude remains and I have a strong attachment to the place without ever being blind to its limitations. In fact, there never was an opportunity to move on and, until after the political change in 1994, I never tried.

My time in Johannesburg was not long enough for me to really gauge the character of the University of the Witwatersrand in any depth. The rhetoric that was characteristic of the institution seemed familiar enough to me from my experience of the US, Britain and Britain's former colonies in Africa. However, as I gradually found out, South African higher education was fairly distinctive, quite apart from the notorious feature of racial segregation. By the mid-1980s there were universities that were supposed to cater for each of the four national 'races' as well as those located in the more substantial Bantustans.

The white English-speaking institutions saw themselves as the cream of the crop. In reality, they had had a distinctly colonial character in the earlier decades of their foundation. South Africa was a country with a population sizeable and rich enough to require a regular stream of engineers, doctors and lawyers who needed university institutions in order to qualify (and to obtain degrees recognised in the Anglosphere, above all in Britain). A very small number of individuals – liberals in the South African mould, a few of whom were radicalised – studied Africans and their ways. This was Bantu studies, later dubbed African studies. Thus Natal had a small African studies department which included several anthropologists. By contrast, sociology, with its more universal claims, was newer and less developed, growing out of social work. After the efforts of the brain trust assembled by General Smuts, including E.G. Malherbe, the future University of Natal vice-chancellor, and the establishment in 1940 of the Council for Scientific and Industrial Research, science received strong support in every sense from the government. This was essentially respected by the National Party when it came to power in 1948. You could not perhaps compare the science world in South Africa with that in the US or even Britain in wealth or prestige, but it did probably compare very decently with, say, Canada or Australia although it was always relatively smaller than was desirable.

By contrast, the social sciences and humanities were weak sisters. In the popular eye, there was little reason to study these subjects. The most talented or ambitious teachers tended to be foreigners passing through or were South Africans en route to overseas. My impression was that there was even a longer tradition in which serious intellectually minded individuals were expected to leave the pleasant world of the colonies for Oxbridge or London. Especially after 1960, for many it was no longer an acceptably pleasant world. In any case, the South African equivalent to what the British call the chattering classes or the French the BBs, bourgeois bohemians, largely nestled in or not too far away from the universities, was and still is very small.

At first, the humanities could at least hope to count on enrolling future teachers, but the popularity of school teaching diminished as time went on and it lost respectability compared with accountancy or actuarial science, the dreary university gold standard. Since student numbers were the basis for hiring staff, often the biggest humanities department was Classics, because the fusty medicine and law programmes demanded that students take a minimum of Latin. The dominance in real terms of the subjects that offered students direct access to jobs became more pronounced after the universities grew (not that they were very large) in the 1970s. In my faculty we had to deal mostly with students who did not really know what they wanted to study and were in fact very weak. The South African school system, very old-fashioned, led to matric exams for university entrance that were of a poor standard compared with British A-levels or good SAT scores in the US.[1] As university education spread for people of colour, there developed an undercurrent of white feeling that you needed to get your children a degree so they would continue to be able to compete and, indeed, more than compete and, by the 1980s, emigrate to Britain, the US, Australia or Canada, where their inexpensive South African degrees were recognised.

Despite the creaky and old-fashioned school curricula that were dominant, it remained true that students needed to study only three years for a degree, and in the final year only needed to take two subjects, their 'majors'. Only a tiny proportion went on to the fourth, Honours year. In the South African system at its best, students were in a sense prepared to respond systematically to particular questions, just as they were encouraged, if bright, to take up debating. However, they read very little, had little access to general knowledge of real sophistication, and there was very little equivalent to the term papers and long essays which American students start to do, often on topics of their own choosing, from the later years of elementary school onwards and which often form the basis of university grades in advanced classes. By this token, I would have described only the final major year as a real university-level set of courses. The majority of our students just wanted a degree and were happy to have the economic history major, which only functioned in the final two years, with the lowest class of marks that could get you through.

These students were in general uncomplaining and passive. I remember being very amused when a poll was taken of student satisfaction with Howard College, which was the usual name for the University of Natal Durban (UND) campus, and the main negative response concerned the irritating seasonal presence of ants out of doors during lunch hour. My impression was that undergraduate education, which had been life-changing for me, was for them comparable to going to the dentist – unpleasant but probably necessary. The boys were much happier on the sports fields. Standards were such that the great majority could expect to get a degree. The large bottom group also included some male scapegraces who exhibited their sense of individuality and rebellion by doing no work (or perhaps cheating in some way) and failed.

My impression on arrival in 1985 was that you could compare the humanities and social science network of teaching staff in Durban at best to that of the most modest of American state colleges, with some university features rather irregularly added on. There were a number of departments (Zulu, Philosophy, French, Linguistics, Speech and Drama) that were one-man shows although allowed to award PhDs. There were full professors who had never written a research paper or taken a higher degree and academics who were at best suited to be devoted high school teachers. The university disbursed a fair number of hobby PhDs. For example, I was faced with a woman with a Kenya settler background and no doubt good family connections in the business world, wanting to submit a PhD on Kenyan history, which consisted simply of paraphrasing the chief Nairobi newspaper's articles over some years. She was blissfully ignorant of contemporary African historiography and had not the faintest idea of or interest in what I had written on the subject. On my watch, I made sure that she had serious examiners and, of course, that was the end of this ridiculous thesis. However, the vice-chancellor informed me that I mustn't do this again! Fortunately, there were no more hobby PhDs in economic history. I also remember that in my first classes on African subjects, the white students cheerfully wrote up twenty-year-old material from late-colonial sources – using the present tense.

The library was still quaintly located in the narrow upper floors of Memorial Tower Block while the present facility (which made a huge difference once completed) was under construction. The chief librarian was a Miss Van der Linde, daughter of a former mayor of Bloemfontein, who presided over a forbidden books section kept under lock and key. The wonderful home of Killie Campbell with its collection of books, artwork and other critical resources concerned especially with black life in this part of South Africa was a special property of UND, quite another story, but was still suffering from the leadership of Van der Linde's henchwoman. One committee I did sit on concerned the governance of Killie Campbell, and the struggle to get the lady in charge to do some work was a tedious and long one.

The university had separately managed humanities and social science faculties, and I chose to stay in humanities as my home faculty. To some extent this reflected my own background but it was also a reaction to the incestuous and, at best, merely superficially liberal nature of the little crowd of social science professors. Much of the humanities faculty was also tedious but the larger size meant that I felt more able to function in this setting. It was typical that Economics seceded from the social sciences and signed up with Commerce, purely because it was a richer faculty regardless of intellectual value or importance. What counted was student numbers – and Commerce was where one could find the mounting number of students who merely sought a well-paying job after graduation.

I held little interest in governance in this kind of institution and I suppose the academics would not have liked or trusted me. I was consigned to committees dealing with the likes of the Killie Campbell Library or the University Press, where I did feel some sense of engagement. The truth is that I quite liked the job of teaching. I enjoyed the classroom. I was happy to classify the students with grades as well as getting to know the more interesting ones, and I was not at all unconventional in my ideas about standards even if I was inclined to reward interesting but eccentric cases.

I was perfectly happy to eliminate or fail students with miserable track records, to me an important task for universities. Moreover, I didn't like rewarding students because of their political proclivities per se.

The dominant culture of the university was liberal. I remember the shrewd vice-chancellor, Pete Booysen, once or twice leading us round the top of Howard College in an orderly and completely meaningless little parade as a supposed demonstration against one or other violation of academic freedom. As a result, one rarely got genuinely right-wing, government-supporting students in one's class, but I tried hard to mark according to quality alone and not whether my own views were getting support.

So far, what I have suggested might have been a deadly if materially acceptable setting, but actually that would give an incorrect impression. There were a growing number of politically alive and intellectually open young people entering a number of departments. The Sociology people, although in my view mostly mediocre intellectually, were a left-wing bunch with strong trade union connections and a separate industrial sociology programme. The most interesting departments, far as they were from my background, were Planning, with a professor, Mike Kahn, who happened to be the first cousin of the historian Shula Marks, and Music under the guidance of Chris Ballantine. It was pretty easy to get to know individuals across department and even faculty lines. My first important friendships were with individuals I would never have met in another setting – Jeff McCarthy, a young geographer, Mike Sutcliffe, a planner who would one day become the Durban city manager, Jeremy Grest, an SOAS MA graduate in the African Studies Department, and Rob Morrell, who arrived at the same time as I did to teach history at the parallel university set up for Indians. There were also others, and they were very interested in Marxist ideas and formed a social as well as intellectual community with which I was very much at home. Only in high school and then in Oxford was there any comparison in my life. It was a rich social integument that kept my weekends very pleasantly occupied.

This left community nonetheless was smaller than in Johannesburg. It also had an unusual character because of the historical weakness of the ANC. The Inkatha movement, which controlled the KwaZulu Bantustan and which was led by Mangosuthu Buthelezi of the Zulu royal family, had a presence and an independent basis of support far beyond that of any other Bantustan-based black political party. On the one hand, Inkatha had broken decisively with the ANC over the armed struggle and completely alienated the radical youth attracted to opposition. However, it also rejected the idea of Bantustan independence, supported development programmes and had good relations with much of the more liberal-minded provincial white elite, including that at the university. At first sight, it was a socially conservative force (although, in my opinion now, with a base not very different from that of the ANC) that seemed prepared to block social transformation, if anything; but, with hindsight, its willingness to take on the ANC created neutral ground that would not have existed had either been entirely dominant. This made for a great deal of space, of independence for somebody like me who wanted to steer clear of the ANC but engage with left ideas in the classroom and even outside. Nobody forgot the fate of the charismatic Rick Turner, a politics lecturer with an unusual background in philosophy, who had studied in France. Turner was banned but he showed no sign of ANC adherence. Nevertheless, a hit squad, perhaps intending only to scare him, shot and killed him after firing through the door of his home in 1979. The atmosphere of fear this spread had only partly dissipated when I arrived five years later.

The other factor in Durban was the strength of the independent trade unions, which had already captured my sympathy. Durban as a port attracted industry, particularly industry using foreign raw materials and taking advantage of plentiful cheap labour and protected national markets. Several major emerging unions, notably the chemical, metal and textile workers, had national headquarters in Durban and many organised workers. I made friends with some white and also Indian organisers, often very bright individuals who had reached research level as students and were very comfortable with intellectuals; they were people who lived on a pittance by white South African standards, with heads full of politics and amazing drive. They had a big influence on my thinking about South African politics as I engaged with their debates and problems. The still-largest union federation, Cosatu, the Congress of South African Trade Unions, was in fact born on our campus in 1985. I remember well the post-deliberation celebrations when the Durban-based new general secretary, Jay Naidoo, later a cabinet minister, was hoisted high in the air at the party in the gymnasium of the Student Union.

Figure 11.2: On a visit Bill Hansen joined me at a rally to celebrate the birth of Cosatu, 1985

In addition, it was easy to get to meet anti-apartheid professionals, doctors, lawyers, journalists and so on. There was a community based on the need for separation both from the mainstream values of white Durban and from the partisan requirements of the ANC – almost a necessity if you wanted to stay out of gaol and avoid the threat of deportation. Of course, it had close links to sister communities in other cities. Rob Morrell has put together material with somewhat different ideas and orientation on this fraternity. He was a long-time colleague in Durban and a close friend. I put some pressure on him in a crucial late period in talking about myself and my life, which caused a temporary rift, but it was very useful in my reaching the point where I could write as I have done in these pages. Rob has focused lately on the changing group of men who played touch rugby on a university sports field: for some just a form of recreation, for others a kind of social club, and for me also a badge of collegial masculinity, of which I had very little experience when I was young.

He has also suggested this as the background that made possible the creation of an independent, politically engaged journal, *Transformation*, which still exists and which I helped to edit. My co-founders were Mike Morris, a trade unionist who needed a steadier and larger income and thus became a new university colleague, and Gerry Maré. Gerry came with the experience of working on another journal from his time at Wits, *Work in Progress*, which was an important initiative but did not survive the shift to democratic government. A member of the Sussex University 'gang of four', Mike had a brilliant mind, independent and frustrated with the fixed doctrines that seemed politically too dominant in Cape Town. His academic writing is generally excellent but he had little liking for, or patience with, conventional academic practice. Mike, more than anyone else in Durban, changed me politically. I began to see that, while it certainly had pitfalls, it might be possible to be an effective practical politician without abandoning principles. This, I would say, made me increasingly different from the principled academic Marxists of the US, the *Kathedermarxists* as they were long ago called in Germany, who were better by far on ideas than on politics. We soon took on as editor a lecturer from the University of Durban-Westville (UDW), a quite separate institution established for the Indian minority, which was considerably more substantial than the black African equivalents in the country. It employed many white lecturers and was also increasingly attracting radical young academics or postgraduate students. This was the case for Vishnu Padayachee, who had already looked me up at the ASI in Johannesburg.

A very healthy and welcome part of life at Howard College was the willingness of many of us to interrelate with UDW and to forge ties with other professionals. This was dramatically unlike US academic life. I think one can argue that academic institutions are structured precisely so as to create the silos in which people live their often quite alienated professional lives. It was very good for me, especially given my wide range of interests, that this was so readily overcome, and I could always look beyond the institution. Unlike other ephemeral initiatives that have frustrated me, *Transformation* has so far been a long-term success, although I think it has struggled to keep up the level of excitement that we were able to sustain in the 1980s. I also initiated a cross-department, autonomous set of late-afternoon seminars, which was another focus of cultural and intellectual life that made the university a more interesting place.

If I shift the subject from colleagues to students, the picture is also a more mixed one than I have indicated above. Just as at Wits, there was a minority of perhaps ten per cent of the student body who were focused on the mounting crisis in South Africa. Some of these people were simply interested in getting their inexpensive degree and, given the outlook as they saw it for South Africa, emigrating to safer pastures. There were always a few, normally boys, who were forced to do well to make it to the next level and qualify for a law degree.[2] The rest often included the elected student leadership and typically were highly politicised and committed to fighting apartheid. It is clearer with hindsight that one must grasp that 'fighting apartheid' itself was not a uniform idea, and the differences went beyond the most obvious one of support of or opposition to the armed struggle and aligned organisation and activity. It was also, for whites, a range that existed between wanting to honour liberal ideals, which could go together very comfortably with a business career and belonging to the upper middle class, and genuine interest in a radical restructuring of society; between just assuring the right of everyone legally to the vote, access to housing and schools and the like, and creating a situation where the huge economic and social differences, cavernous in South Africa, were highlighted and denounced in the interests of a far less unequal and far more integrated whole. However, at this time, these were just nuances. The enemy at hand was clearly the state and those allied to it and prepared to do its bidding.

Politics as well as academic achievement thus meant that I got to know many of the most interesting students on campus. Relating to them was for most left-wing lecturers, and to a large extent also for me, more exciting and more telling than organising syllabi and marking fairly, although I tried to make sure our courses were well taught and reliably administered for everybody.

The truth was that, after my long years of professional insecurity, I was not going to be the one to make defiant speeches denouncing the immorality of the Pretoria authorities. If humanly possible, I did not want to be thrown out of the country and have my Durban life brought to a principled but disastrous end. I made it my business, even on the telephone, to indicate that I had sympathies with the ANC and was not its enemy at all but at the same time that I had no interest either in a secret existence doing their work for them. On the other hand, I was happy to do whatever I could for the new unions. Here, too, there were limits. Unlike other academics with these sympathies, I was not really able, given my background, to shut up and simply preach whatever line on whatever subject was current policy. I just lacked that sense of political discipline. As a result, I was not taken into any inner circles and was never even encouraged, as I would have liked, to involve myself in night school teaching for shop stewards. In the end, I felt that the work I did do as an academic and through the circles I frequented was probably what I did best. My sociological understanding of the black working class and the unions that emerged by and for them was superficial.

In 1986 (I think) a student of mine named Brad Stacey went on a mission of sabotage. He set fire to the office of Lawrence Schlemmer, perhaps the campus individual most associated with Inkatha (he left Durban soon afterwards), and of the notorious reactionary Professor Frederick Clifford-Vaughan, who had come down from Rhodesia to succeed Rick Turner in Politics and who was eventually dismissed for secretly meddling with another staff member's papers. Sadly in this case, the whole Politics Department in Shepstone Building near to us was badly damaged. Stacey skipped town and joined Umkhonto we Sizwe (MK), the armed wing of the ANC. This was true of another student as well, an Indian chap, Abba Omar.[3] For both Stacey and Omar, skipping town occurred just after I had started to organise seminars for them to discuss their research, so I found this a rather extreme response to a conventional academic demand! I was questioned about Brad by the security police in my office, and fortunately I knew very little, although I liked this intelligent and obviously idealistic boy very much. I did lie a bit, however, to cover him. Later on, Brad tried to hijack an aeroplane in Tanzania in order to escape from MK and he went through a tough time in prison as a result. After that I lost the trail. The most I ever did illegally was to allow Omar to have a meeting or two in my house while I was in the office during the day. If truth be told, while I recall one security agent in a class of mine, I never got into the least trouble in the last apartheid years.

Figure 11.3: Mass protest before the Durban City Hall, March 1989

On the issue of security, I should also mention something in quite a different category for most purposes. After the life I had led, I was very eager to own a house that could finally be my home, to fix it up as I liked, to entertain and have visitors, and hopefully one with some green space added. I gave notice on the temporary housing I was allocated, a flat in Shepstone Building, after finding a house where I proposed to move when my six months in the university flat were up. I was greeted with the news that I was supposed to move out almost immediately and accused of threatening to disobey orders. I was summoned to the flat of the housing man, an ex-military chap, where Professor Colin Webb, an historian who was a deputy principal, was present. It turned out that this man had indeed written a letter asking me to move out a month early, but to his considerable embarrassment, it turned out that he had neglected to send it. That was the last I heard of him. This little story also illustrates the informal way the pompous and not very effective bureaucracy operated. It gave me in turn great leeway as a head of department, and I was able to serve as such for three five-year periods – very different from the life of an untenured assistant professor in the US, a position I no longer had to think about.

As to the house, what I bought was a bungalow built in the 1970s on three levels towards the top of a hillside. It was only four minutes' drive from my parking bay at the university, which was important given my propensity to sleep very late by South African standards. Below the house was quite a lot of increasingly wild land as well as two lychee trees, which I harvested. There was a separate tiny flat at the lowest level, ideal for guests, and next to that a swimming pool. Given that the cost of installing a pool was modest and that during most of the year I spent time in it every afternoon, it was not an outrageous luxury despite the infamy swimming pools had among self-righteous anti-apartheid activists. I tried to minimise the security, I didn't have walls surrounding the property, and the car stayed outside with only a canvas carport cover on top each night.

Best of all was the beautiful view of a large green valley rising above the Umhlatuzana stream. I had a deck built off the lounge on the top level. In later years monkeys would love to come and play on the glass table if I kept quiet and was unnoticeable indoors. Much further on was the huge empty space of Cato Manor. Black shacks had been destroyed here en masse at the end of the 1950s, but neither whites nor Indians had ever wanted to move there in significant numbers, so, despite much degraded vegetation,

Figure 11.4: The deck at my home, 17 Forsdick Road, Durban

this was a wonderful wilderness in the city and its denizens often made their way to the Umhlatuzana and further up into people's gardens. I got a wonderful taste of the natural kingdom of South Africa. Over the years I encountered owls, monitor lizards, mongooses, snakes, several species of frogs and rodents. I also counted over the years more than fifty bird species, including one or two birds of prey. This partly impelled me to become a keen birdwatcher and on weekends I sometimes explored the best places around Durban to encounter unusual species from the very rich wildlife of coastal Natal. Sadly, it would not have been practical to keep a pet as I travelled so often, but this array of winged and two-, four- or more-footed visitors more than made up for it. This was a kind of childhood fantasy come true for me.

In my African years, I have spent much leisure time in game parks and nature reserves. Of many great experiences, the most remarkable of all was a guided hike in 1989 through the Umfolozi-Hluhluwe game park in northern Natal on foot with a ranger who exposed me to the extraordinary richness of birdlife. I remember picking up porcupine quills and looking at a distance from on high at a lion chasing a prospective meal. This expedition overcame my normal urban American sense of timidity and potential danger from exposure to too much nature. Another memorable experience was a canoe trip down the Zambezi in 1992 from Lake Kariba to Mana

Figure 11.5: On holiday on the Zambezi: a crocodile takes down a buffalo, 1992

Figure 11.6: On Bazaruto Island, Mozambique, 1996

Pools, passing numerous elephant and hippopotamus, a huge crocodile gorging on a buffalo, and other memorable sights over five days. These things certainly changed my perceptual horizons considerably.

The first years in Durban were perhaps the slackest for me in scholarly commitment. Of course, I needed to get my courses in order for teaching purposes. But the teaching load was light. Very few of the undergraduates had any interest in going on to further study, even to do the fourth, bridging Honours year, an archaic idea still maintained in South Africa and without which it was hard to discern how much they had achieved as students. I was also in a kind of unquestioned position of authority as head of department, a very new idea for me. The one problem that deserves mentioning in this account was the mental health of my colleague Dan North-Coombes. When Dan took a sabbatical to return to Mauritius and complete his PhD research, he experienced panic attacks of a serious nature and was effectively diagnosed as bipolar. His psychiatrist advised him, perhaps foolishly, to stop research. His now very unstable personality was finally addressed by a heavy drug dose that took over the remainder of his life. He was able to keep on teaching in part because I was able to hire some temporary help, but I found keeping him going a difficult burden and a very depressing one. Dan lived to see the new South Africa created in 1994, a subject of much joy for him, but a couple of years later, while

I was out of the country, he shot himself. By this time, I was, regretfully, ready to have him boarded. Managing this situation was a very new kind of experience for me. I felt especially the absence of his intellectual companionship, which had seemed so very promising, given his interests in slavery, agrarian systems and Asia, and particularly his enthusiasm about China, which complemented my own interests so well. This despite his somewhat romantic take on politics and his very Mauritian concern with race at the boundary line. My first attempt at a replacement was not very successful: I chose a social historian in the hopes that he would focus more on the economy. Also a romantic with a difficult personality, he instead put years into celebrating a minor MK guerrilla's life. Only in the new millennium did I create a little team I enjoyed working with, and my two fellow lecturers, one Canadian and one South African, became close friends. This required opening up a second major in development studies in which I did very little teaching myself.

Slowly I acquired a few postgraduate students, but in most cases (Shireen Hassim, Joe Kelly, Lungisile Ntsebeza, Rob Morrell) they were refugees from other unsatisfactory units and experiences, and they chose topics far not only from my personal interests but also from my remit as an economic historian. An exception, very much oriented to economic issues, was the UDW academic and my fellow *Transformation* editor, Vishnu Padayachee, whose thesis on South Africa's relations with the international financial bodies such as the International Monetary Fund and the Bank of International Settlements was completed towards the end of the 'old days'. Vishnu has remained a close friend and others too – in fact, most of my PhD students of the past – have remained important contacts and associates. This, too, is unlike what one would expect in a normal academic setting.

I did formulate a research project after a few years. It led to my book on the Indian working class, *Insiders and Outsiders*. A few Indian friends or acquaintances have done me the tribute of saying how well I captured their sense of historical change and experience. Vishnu's advice was invaluable. However, while I was able to capture the essential line that interested me, I think my failure to do extensive interviewing or real social history was a limitation of the project. I wanted to do something different from the available series of ethnographic studies of Indian life in Durban, such as

Fatima Meer's *Portrait of a Minority* as well as earlier books. What fascinated me was that, in the face of a high level of white hostility and legal impediments, Indians chose for the most part to stay in South Africa after the abolition of indenture and despite the blandishments of the state, which wanted them all sent away. Under segregation and then apartheid, on average they improved their situation increasingly, although it is true that after 1960 important reforms placed them in a favourable position compared with blacks. Thus instead of emphasising their anti-apartheid credentials, I focused on social mobility and, in a sense, assimilation to South African ways (conversion to Christianity, shift to English as home language) that worked practically. Through this book, I developed by contrast a sharper sense of the causes of relative African poverty and material failure as a particular complex not explained entirely by white oppression – different from what the usual anti-apartheid literature ever allowed for. I doubt, though, that many African readers have ever read the book and considered this message.

Simultaneously I became more and more preoccupied with the Economic Trends (earlier, Labour and Economic Research) Group. Its director was Steve Gelb, who came back from Canada with a PhD at the same time I arrived at Wits but then moved on to a research job in Durban at UDW. Alec Erwin, the future cabinet minister, was part of the important metal workers' union. Through him we liaised with Cosatu, and in effect the Cosatu federation stood behind this project. Here I gradually got up to speed in understanding twentieth-century South African economic history and political economy and the problems the country was facing at that level. I owe a lot here to Steve and other members of the group, such as Jean Leger, who pioneered the idea of tacit worker knowledge, by looking at mine accidents, and Mike de Klerk, one of the first writers on the dilemmas of farm workers, whose numbers were rapidly decreasing. Dave Kaplan at the University of Cape Town wrote incisively on the problematique of South African secondary industry. This has been foundational to my later work. Despite one article on the changing situation in the gold mines in a Gelb-edited collection, my designated interest in gold as a key research area never developed further. What I wrote didn't transpire. The very expensive and technically challenging plans to plough ever deeper under the earth for more gold have on the whole not happened, as the price of gold fell. I also felt that Durban was not an appropriate locus for writing about gold mining. To push ahead slightly, when I got the first call from ANC government-related people to come up at short notice to a Johannesburg meeting on gold mining, I ignored it and decided that this was not for me.

Very few Economic Trends stalwarts remained academics. The glory and, if I dare say it, the money were to lie in a host of possibilities, with various levels of autonomy, in working for the new state after 1994. My own idea was to remain an academic but to push towards a research agenda that involved the problems of a post-apartheid economy. This meant a much more intense focus on economic history, not just left-wing history. I would not say that I have never served in any government-related capacity, but basically I stayed out of this world while often having a first-hand knowledge of and sometimes a continued friendship with those in the thick of it.

In 1992 I was named a University Fellow, an honour the university created, of little substance and almost totally in abeyance now, for senior academics with good research histories, mainly scientists. I can claim that at the ceremony the first person to applaud me on stage was the new honorary degree holder, Nelson Mandela. At the time, the universities all clamoured to find ways to gain legitimacy with the coming new national leadership and, above all, with the apparently saintly Mandela. Still it was a great moment. Two years earlier I had gone home at lunchtime to hear the momentous F.W. de Klerk speech freeing Mandela and opening the road to the legalisation of the ANC and its Communist allies, abolishing various apartheid laws and moving to initiate an open negotiations forum. Two years later I sat with Jeremy Grest and his wife, Judith Shier, watching Mandela's inauguration as president.

It seems important to me to discuss to some degree how the new regime struck me. I was unsurprised at the February 1990 bombshell. There were many hints that the National Party was desperate to find a solution and, with President P.W. Botha gone, was inching towards the De Klerk decision. Nor could I see another way out of the conflictual and increasingly violent situation that prevailed, as the ANC was very far from being able to win a military victory. Indeed, at that level it was pretty thoroughly defeated, and humiliatingly so. However, the government victory at that level was very costly and did not get around the problem of sanctions and the growing demands of the powerful business community for breaking out of isolation. The Bantustan solution and the tricameral parliament solution had both failed; clearly the whole 'non-white' population was growing insubordinate and extremely restless. The state had little to deliver to them under the existing system.

It is still something of a mystery to me how the ANC, given its feebleness in the 1960s and even the 1970s, could make the comeback that it did, but it was clear by the subsequent decade, and once I had moved to South Africa, that it really had no serious rival in black politics. Given the violence of youth action in key areas (Transvaal townships and Zululand), Cosatu adhesion and the success the party would have in buying the allegiance of conservative rural people and their leaders, including most of those involved in running the Bantustans, it was not going to lose a national election. The 'liberal' opposition was unconvincing in providing a plausible commitment, beyond deracialisation, towards creating a more equal society. The ANC had the support of virtually all my friends and it held the promise of redistribution without bringing the country to ruin.

The negative side for me was the black nationalist element in its thinking, such as the noxious idea that white South Africa was to be dismissed as an equivalent to colonialism – 'colonialism of a special type' – a convenient term for some time. However, I understood from my life elsewhere in Africa that black South Africans were rarely interested in integration; they had the same racialised nationalist impulse as further north. It was perfectly understandable, but the nationalists offered no alternative that was not merely destructive. Moreover, their often-expressed interest in inequality and the like was shot through with a pretty crude obsession with empowerment, not the creation of a social democratic or deracialised society except on their own terms. In addition, there simply was very little expertise in running a modern society or organising a transformation among ANC ranks. This was a revolutionary movement with poorly educated cadres, perhaps relying in the past on using a Soviet example that was highly outmoded. It had very little purchase on people with skills and ideas, most of whom were of the wrong colour for the ANC.

The few individuals encouraged to take up economic policy studies right at the end of the struggle came back with the new assumption that neo-liberal thinking was the way forward, with no real alternatives or even qualifications. This was apparent to me in April 1990 when, together with other Economic Trends members, I was invited to meet with ANC repre- sentatives in Harare. To put it mildly, there was nothing to be excited about at the policy level. This helped me decide to marginalise my involvement there, for which I was probably too unreliable in any case.

In the years after 1994, the ANC did a lot of good. In Mandela's time it crucially blocked and made impossible a coup by the police or military, eager to bring back the past. It created good labour legislation. It equal- ised pensions and supported the creation of a child support grant. When AIDS spread like wildfire, more and more individuals received disability grants and, after the ousting of President Thabo Mbeki, benefited from the widespread and gratis diffusion ('roll-out') of the necessary drugs to keep people going. A very slowly diminishing quarter of the population receive these grants.

In an age when public housing was pushed back and was even vanishing in the rich countries, the state constructed hundreds of thousands of little houses, secure, electrified and with indoor plumbing, as hand-out gifts to people. Despite all one can say about gender and patriarchy, a great many of the beneficiaries of all this were women and female-headed households. Women were promoted to high office in large numbers, a rather different story but still in principle a good thing. Under the new constitution, cre- ated by pro-ANC liberal lawyers, capital punishment was abolished and homosexual marriage legalised, in both cases clearly against the wishes of most South Africans. The tax system posed a considerable burden on the affluent, comparable to Europe on the whole and far more serious than in America. You could not complain about elections being fixed or the media being shackled in what became genuinely a democracy. And, inevitably, there was lots and lots of affirmative action for positions where power and money were at stake.

There was also much that was negative or that at least blocked further transformation. Much of the legislative customary system that ruled in the Bantustans was maintained, together with a respectful attitude to often greedy and acquisitive 'chiefs'. The widely diffused but qualitatively miser- able educational system, very poorly oriented towards building construc- tive modern habits, skills and ideas, stayed in place, partly at the behest of useless teachers casting about for patronage jobs and promotions.

In my more recent research on development states, I applied to South Africa the model several writers that influenced me had considered in East Asia. A fundamental aspect of the developmental state has been close cooperation between business and the government in Japan, Korea, Taiwan and, now in a different mode, China. In South Africa the relationship with business, apart from pressure for affirmative action executive jobs, was poor, owing to the mentality on both sides of the fence. It is understandable that the ANC would like to see a dynamic new class of black capitalists. But the class created by Black Economic Empowerment structures remains very dependent on state patronage and tends to cleave close to the old mining sector, notably in coal. Dynamic ideas about economic growth were absent beyond vague projections. The naive commitment of Mandela, Mbeki & Co. to a free trade universe, the very reverse of the old sanctions policy, did nothing for the myriad of low-skilled black workers. Unemployment quickly rose to huge levels with few parallels in the world and this trend was coupled with the shift at work to precarious forms of employment for many. The mines and farms in particular shed plenty of labour.

The ANC simply did not know what to do about this. It had a range of well-meant policies but they were often contradictory and never very well coordinated or dominant. Keeping the ship afloat in the eyes of foreign investors was always a priority. The blockages to developing a dynamic growth-oriented economy, in my view, are powerful and unlikely to change in the foreseeable future, ensuring slow growth or stagnation, with complete dependence on raw material prices. What is termed load shedding to maintain electricity lines at all has become a regular feature of the 'minerals–energy complex'.

Nor does the party know how to knit white and black together, and it tolerates and even encourages by implication the perpetuation of the social-cultural silos that characterise South African society. These attitudes and practices are loosening at the edges, something I try to celebrate in my writing wherever I see the start of a genuinely more mixed kind of society, but there is, to put it mildly, a long way to go.

And affirmative action in the form of so-called cadre deployment, largely connected to race (not that the few Coloured or white ANC loyalists were left out), often promoted stupid, incompetent and corrupt comrades, of whom there were very many. Given the absence of a business class in black ranks and the slow process involved in substantial retraining, the power of the state to intervene has meant, for instance in the running of key parastatal corporations, high levels of corruption as well as incompetence. The subsidence of the state into a pear-shaped structure, allowing for the payment of as many actors' family school fees, medical expenses and show-off consumer items as possible, is very familiar to any serious observer of independent Africa. South Africa, different only in its greater economic complexity and human diversity, is no exception. Without economic growth, there is no possibility of equalisation, even of opportunity, on the terms of the middle class, and this may eventually destroy the life chances of much of that class, as happened demonstrably in Mugabe's Zimbabwe. Whites have largely fled Zimbabwe and any sense of 'colonialism' being in power must be gone (there are still some fusty survivals of old ways of doing things in the bureaucracy broadly conceived) but at the expense of GNP falling below the level of Zambia. In South Africa, white males continue to form a very large proportion of those leaving school with real competence in maths and science. What can one achieve with a policy of trying to exclude them significantly from positions of responsibility? This is a dilemma which fine talk about non-racialism or social cohesion fails to resolve.

To sum up, my view of ANC governance is a mixed bag. I am not a voter but I would probably vote for them, for lack of an alternative rather than from any enthusiasm for them. Left ideas are important to me still. I think it will be a losing battle for a middle power like South Africa to defy globalising trends in world capitalism; we have to learn to go with the tide in crucial respects. However, we have to be alert to the constant need to mitigate and sometimes address substantially the consequences for the mass of people. There is no alternative to clearing out a lot of crap that sits in the heads of the population, very much including the black masses, and pointing them in a modernist direction.

I am always delighted to see a black South African doing a great job at a substantial level, but whether people at that level are one colour or another means very little to me at bottom. This is not an approach which is very fashionable anywhere, but as I age, I feel more capable of expressing myself as I really think. This does put me at odds, perhaps sadly, with all the idealists who reified the idea of liberation, are horrified at the presence of corruption divorced from an understanding of the system as a whole, who feel betrayed and like to cling to catch-all terms like neo-liberalism as the source of all evil, or think that the transition of 1994 was some calculated sell-out. One old friend who shall be nameless actually told me that South Africa has 'disappointed him'. He left for Europe, and in fact many of those who gave of themselves selflessly to contribute to the downfall of the old regime and the creation of a new one have emigrated, encouraged their children to leave, and vote for the opposition Democratic Alliance along-side the great majority of non-black Africans. This reaction is carefully not registered anywhere, and I try to avoid it myself.

I should balance the scales a bit with some more positive comments. It is a relief and pleasure, of course, to be able to deal normally with people of all backgrounds and colours. I look at the US of Donald Trump and feel very pleased not to be there or among those who like what he has to say. In the current Covid-19 pandemic, I have been interested to see some new ideas come forward. The head of Eskom, the electricity utility, has for the first time discussed the importance of favouring renewables in energy. Maybe this unpredictable crisis will have a Schumpeterian effect, killing the old weighing us down and encouraging the birth of the new. That is certainly what South Africa needs.

No doubt my views have been reinforced by my personal experiences in 1994 and after. At one level, we were relatively swamped by a huge crime wave. This has gone down somewhat but it remains high. It was marked by the tendency of many criminals to go in for gratuitous vio-lence, reflecting deep-seated hatred held from the old social situation. Such violence makes an ageing body anxious. My pleasure in accessing the old-fashioned city centre, once replete with shops, restaurants and cinemas that I liked to use, has had to be curbed. The centre of Durban is still very full of people and has all the big monopoly chain stores, but ser-vices catering to white middle-class people have disappeared. For this you must drive to suburbia. I have largely abandoned going to the beach by myself or taking walks, often with the object of birdwatching, as solitary parks and nature reserves are not safe enough. And I have been mugged, as have most people like me, once. My old house was broken into and we once lost a set of new computers in the department office before they were even unpacked.

There were two larger changes, however, which do require detailing before I complete my narrative. In the transition years, my social life gradually disappeared. One colleague and much-liked friend after the other stayed in the country but moved to Cape Town or Johannesburg, often abandoning academic life altogether. Union headquarters shifted to the Highveld, too, as factories closed down and most organisers became bureaucrats of one sort or another, sometimes very well remunerated. The tendency grew to see success, which transcended the race line, as something that happened in those two centres, with Durban more like a provincial second-rank city suitable only for an early career phase. Moreover, the need for left-minded people to stick together also largely dissipated. With more money, it was desirable and possible to mend domestic fences and pursue more family-centred private lives. The parties, the expeditions down the coast or up to the Berg, passed into memory. For me, given who I am, this was the main cause of a noticeable and significant depression which got me down for many months, a sense of aimlessness and anomie completely the opposite of my earlier, pre-1990 experience of life in South Africa.

My idea that the university would start to attract many young people eager to be involved in promoting social and economic change in the 'new South Africa' was itself naive. Within months of the De Klerk speech to Parliament freeing Mandela and lifting the ban on the ANC and the Communist Party, the conventional white student body we had been teaching in the department, which had been gently declining in size for some years, began to disappear. Already in 1991, the enrolment of majors halved; white parents lost interest in their offspring obtaining South African university arts degrees. What we got in return in the first years was a far smaller number of very poor black students who either failed or just about got a fifty per cent mark, the lowest possible grade for passing, which satisfied them. They were even quite a bit worse than their mediocre white predecessors and basically unequipped for university-level studies. Only the occasional interesting individual entered our doors now.

As I have suggested earlier, this prompted me to come up with the idea of us offering a second major in development studies. Before his suicide, I persuaded myself that Dan would have to go. On this basis I was able to hire a new member of staff and the results, with one exception, were ultimately quite positive. That exception was my role as the one who still wanted to teach economic history and, to boot, from a perspective that was global, not parochial and national, and genuinely committed to the study of history. Intellectually this was complicated by the take-over of economic history in most countries by a sterile, deductive, quantitative project of little interest to me.[4] I myself still had just a tiny number of students beyond my contribution to an introductory course. Often I lectured to just two or three at a time, a strange situation.

In 1996, moreover, the University of Natal appointed as vice-chancellor the first-ever woman to occupy such a post, Brenda Gourley, a business studies academic with no record of research or even a research degree. With Gourley, the cold and, to me, hateful wind of Thatcherism blew in. Among other 'reforms', retirement at sixty was introduced, the normal forms of staff self-government were eliminated or marginalised in favour of an alien 'line management' system so called, and we were forced into large, intellectually meaningless entities called Schools. It became possible to dismiss even long-serving academics if their services were deemed redundant or ineffectual. For a time, I wondered if I should not try to get out of this system. However, after a few brief trial letters which got nowhere, I abandoned this idea. I felt a bit embarrassed at the idea that I could thrive

Figure 11.7: The Economic History Department at UKZN: Harald Witt, myself and David Moore (seated); John Karumbidza, our PhD student; Debbie Boertje, our secretary; and Buntu Siwisa (standing)

in apartheid South Africa yet not adjust to its successor, but the reality is that I briefly experienced once again that sense of being unwanted, either at the other South African universities or elsewhere.

I have to admit in retrospect that Gourley was very shrewd. She understood very well what middle-class white Natalians wanted in a university and was able, in the Mandela and early Mbeki years, to balance this very skilfully against the dictates of the post-apartheid government. She made a few affirmative action administrative appointments of people with little competence but in situations where they could not do much harm. Natal also benefited from the presence of numerous very competent Indians who could ably fill substantial academic roles. In my view, they have been the salvation at executive level of the tertiary education system, even nationally, so far.

With time I also adjusted to this regime despite my unbusinesslike nature and I have to admit that by the time Gourley retired, the humanities and social science part of the university had greatly improved and university standards were much more serious than twenty years earlier. Development studies did bring us some decent South African students who trickled back to our premises. Indeed, in the later Gourley years, even our undergraduate enrolments improved in quantity and quality although, since I was the one who carried the non-South African part of the economic history programme, I had mixed feelings about the fact that my teaching was for me largely a classroom escape from South Africa even while mostly staying at home in Durban.

In time, my own problem was in a sense solved by a series of involvements in research projects and teaching. My job was regularised in 2004 on unconventional lines despite the stupid new retirement age, with its presumption of collective ineffectiveness at sixty.[5] I was able to secure a one-year-contract part-time appointment while taking my pension. This was then renewed on a nonsensical 'mentoring' basis for three years thanks to the help of Raphael de Kadt, who had become head of the Politics School. I was still employed as a one-off to teach that postgraduate course which had become my main activity at the university, in 2009, my sixty-fifth year, after which I ceased paid work there.

Gradually, I figured out even before then some new ways to operate and survive that fitted the new university culture in the new century. I got involved as partner-member through an old friend, originally based in Johannesburg but now at UDW – Doug Hindson – in a generously funded urban research programme involving the Ivory Coast and France. As UDW imploded, we got the moneys transferred to UND, for which I gained some kudos. In the course of the project I made good friends with several French academics and was eventually appointed as an adviser to the French development programme for joint research with African universities, the main source of PhD awards in France for African students, and became a French bureaucrat, commuting to Paris and travelling in Africa, for some years. When I thought of my beginnings as a French speaker in Lake View High School, this seemed like a grand achievement. I also very much enjoyed the comparative angle, which allowed me to travel to Abidjan in the Ivory Coast, where I made Ivorian and French friends. The programme was at best very uneven, one of a series of rather forlorn French efforts to establish long-term ties with African institutions in anglophone countries, although we salvaged it to a small extent, but I learnt a lot from my participation.

Through the good offices of the sociologist Ari Sitas, I taught a course for a roaming group of German-initiated students from all over the world in an English-language master's course in what was called the Global Studies Programme (in which I was avoided by the very few South African student participants). This brought me in touch each year with very bright students from many countries, notably in eastern Europe, Latin America and Asia, many of whom went on to get PhDs. It was a fabulous learning experience for me, and some of these students remained in contact for years. This is also true of a programme which existed until a poor American student got raped in a residence. This programme brought us exchange students from the University of California, and they were a delight. I had the chance to teach bright American students just as I had done intermittently at the start of my career. Later, after they left, I found a few similarly bright Norwegian individuals registered in my class from yet another exchange programme. Finally, the fact that I took a class in the postgraduate Development Studies Programme, which I had helped to plan initially and which was much favoured by Gourley, also brought me some valuable experience. All these were accompanied by a big new commitment to reading in the contemporary development field and attempting to marry this with the contentious development studies literature.

Some of my views can be found in a book published by UKZN Press and edited with my colleague, the environmental historian Harald Witt, called *Development Dilemmas in South Africa*. It then led on to years of thinking about the developmental state and how to apply this idea to South African twentieth-century history. This, too, led to a book which came out late in 2018: *Twentieth Century South Africa: A Developmental History*. I think it is my most accomplished work theoretically.

Some of my post-millennial publications have been directly concerned with South African political economy but a lot have been focused on urban history. I took this up around 2000 because I felt it was an acceptable way of doing economic history that used my real skills. It put me in contact with the impressive group of South African academic urbanists usually clustered in Planning and Geography Departments, and it could tap into my strong visceral and experiential sense of different kinds of African cities. Of course, I also like cities. As a conference at that juncture in London made clear to me, the urban had arrived in African history. The decades of obsession with rural and ethnic Africa were being pushed aside as new realities sank in. I have so far written one short urban book, *The African City: A History*, which I think was quite successful, have cooperated in urban seminars, conferences and student supervision, and had two enjoyable sabbaticals, first in Paris and then in Uppsala, in Sweden, where I widened my knowledge of the literature on African cities substantially. Into the more ethnographic literature often exclusively focused on the 'poor' and thus continuing the usual African studies victimology, I tried to inject political economy and variety into the picture without abandoning Marxist ideas.

Professor Brenda Gourley retired and went off to head the Open University in England with her business school convictions. It is a pity that Gourley lost the battle against the merger with UDW, for a time a very interesting institution but in bad shape owing to a series of generous decisions in recent years. However, I can understand that the minister of education, Kader Asmal, was desperate to save what had become an impossible situation in a place where he had good friends, and he used the merger route as a solution. UDW's problems foreshadow the current university troubles of today everywhere.

Gourley was succeeded by a vengeful black medical researcher with little university experience and no knowledge of the humanities. An intelligent and, in some respects, an impressive individual, Malegapuru Makgoba was clearly very angry at his treatment by Wits, which had brought him back to South Africa in the hopes of getting a cooperative black figurehead in time for political change but then discarded him. He also, by organising the merger of the two Durban universities, brought on board a lot of intellectual dead wood who fitted into the new regime, one that tended to push race first, accelerated affirmative action even when very inappropriate, and destroyed the improvement in quality one could associate with Gourley. One result was the loss to Durban of most of my remaining friends, who were usually able to pick up work in other centres. I tried myself to organise a move to Johannesburg twice, through the University of Johannesburg and Wits, and additionally to establish a closer link with the economic history programme at the University of Cape Town, but all of these initiatives got me nowhere. All the same, Durban is certainly a more relaxing and easier town and it has a good range of necessary services if quite limited intellectual life. Personally, I have made up for this to some extent with a lot of travel, mostly to Europe, where I make new friends, often of another generation. I am fairly at home in Johannesburg and to some degree in London, where I am lucky enough to have generous family of whom I am fond. This moving around has been a learning experience, as I pick up a sense of other countries, systems, generations, even in these not very happy times. I have made an effort to work as a partner and to write with young scholars, sometimes successfully.

I can imagine any reader of this autobiography will pick up my overall disdain for a lot of mainstream wisdom, and resentment and anger that I was passed over again and again in the country in which I was born and raised. However, when I look back, I also realise that the trials and tribulations that followed put me into many interesting, life-shaking experiences far beyond that of the college professor stuck in a small college town somewhere in the US. To some extent it has made me a different person. South Africa is a challenging and sometimes very exciting place, and my level of involvement with it is also something different and surprising when seen from the perspective of my beginnings and training. For this, and the extent to which it allowed me to realise my dreams and put them to work, I must be very grateful.

Notes

Foreword

1 John Lonsdale, 'A Materialist History of Africa: *The Making of Contemporary Africa: The Development of African Society since 1800*. By Bill Freund', *Journal of African History* 26, no. 1 (1985): 122–123.

2 Robert Morrell, 'Touch Rugby, Masculinity and Progressive Politics in Durban, South Africa, 1985–1990', *International Journal of the History of Sport* 34, nos. 7–8 (2017): 619–638.

A Brief Introduction

1 Reproduced by kind permission of the *London Review of Books*.

Chapter 1 The Austrian Past

1 He favoured this spa very much but seems also to have been connected to Franzensbad and at least for one season he tried to establish himself in Karlsbad.

2 This world of super-rich Indian aristocrats is evoked in Edith Leonora Cheltenham's atmospheric memoir, *Highnesses of Hindostan* (London: Grayson and Grayson, 1934) and she does indeed mention princely family members gracing Marienbad among other spas.

3 Given that Jews never name their children after living parents traditionally, this was probably the elder Markus Munk in a related business, presumably unrelated to and differentiated from my great-grandfather; that is what the 'junior' likely denotes. I am very thankful to Jill Steward for uncovering the first Markus Munk in her historical research.

4 A reliable guide to facts and figures is Robert Wistrich, *The Jews of Vienna in the Age of Franz Josef* (Oxford and New York: Oxford University Press, 1989).

5 In András Koerner, *A Taste of the Past: The Daily Life and Cooking of a 19th-Century Hungarian Jewish Homemaker* (Hanover and London: University Press of New England, 2004), a very respectable gentleman is discussed whose great love was not Jewish. Thus, he never married. This kind of situation was no doubt quite common. The book is an excellent evocation of the Hungarian variant of the lifestyle I have tried to capture in these pages.

Chapter 2 The Aftermath of War: A Perilous Modernity

1 Ilse and Georg Waldner, *Das alte Mödling II, 1919–1959* (Vienna: Jugend & Volk, 1994), 31. It only cost 80 groschen to be admitted to the *Stadtbad*, which was opened by a jazz orchestra, a beauty contest and a fashion show: modernity as Austrians conceived it in 1926.

2 Waldner, *Das alte Mödling*, 4.

3 Liesl Gross, 'Edwin Arlington Robinsons längere Versenerzählungen' (PhD diss., University of Vienna, 1936). Critical opinion of these longer poems was actually lukewarm or worse from the start and they were out of print fairly soon and are now largely forgotten.

Chapter 3 The Dark Years

1 See bh.org.il/jewish-spotlight/Austria/modern-era/emigration and diaspora/diaspora of Austrian jews or jta.org/1940/12/30/archive/122000-jewish-emigration-from-austria/since-anschluss.

2 Henceforth my translations.

3 This is now photographed and available inside the brochure that visitors receive: Gabriele Hammermann and Stefanie Pilzweger-Steiner, *Dachau Memorial Site: A Tour* (Munich: Utzverlag, 2017), 40.

Chapter 4 A New Life in America

1 Owing to my father's job, the summer was his busy season and he was unable to get time off work then. As a result we normally drove south in the spring looking for the sun, for mountains and the sea. Actually it was fascinating to explore this part of America as a boy. After a while I got to be the navigator in the car, my parents' sense of direction being limited.

2 I once asked my father in old age whom in public life he had most admired, and his answer was Tito. Tito was not only the father of Communist Yugoslavia but was also born, a contemporary of my father, in what was the old Habsburg empire.

3 You can find the very underpass and its collected dead pigeons in the marvellous short stories set in Chicago by Bette Howland, *Calm Sea and Prosperous Voyage* (Brooklyn: Public Space, 2019), 130. She also provides some remarkable descriptions of Uptown, the neighbourhood I write about, on pp. 145–146.

4 While this detail may seem extreme, in fact I heard and saw equally extraordinary racist comments from my father's side of the family in California. This was part of a striving to 'belong' to the world of Reagan and Trump as opposed to the inclusive side of US politics. Another purveyor of mad racist ideas was the family dentist, whom I would visit in Hyde Park, a bachelor assisted by his unmarried sister, formerly of Berlin. It was horrifying but amusing to listen to his amazing theories of society while imprisoned in the dentist's chair.

Chapter 5 Adolescence: First Bridge to a Wider World

1   In America, there was a very high propensity among east European Jews for the whole family to emigrate to America and a lower propensity for immigrants to return to Europe, compared with almost any other ethnic contingent.

2   Sara Duker's father, Abraham, was a Jewish scholar who edited the journal *Jewish Social Studies*. Other than Stuart's grandfather, I have no knowledge of any other Jewish intellectuals who lived in our neighbourhood.

Chapter 6 As a Student: Chicago and Yale

1   This story is clearly told by Arnold Hirsch, *Making the Second Ghetto: Race and Housing in Chicago 1940–60* (Chicago: University of Chicago Press, 1983). I remember my father was proud of the fact that Marshall Field had until recently held out against tolerating black customers coming to buy in the store; white customers did not like them trying on the same articles of clothing.

2   These perceptions were hardly unique. For a parallel view from slightly later with striking similarities, see David Forbes, 'My Life as a Mind: How I Learned to Stop Worrying and Love the Bomb-University', *University of Chicago Magazine* (April 2002): 26–30.

3   Hobsbawm never left the British Communist Party, but the written evidence of his communications with party leadership after a point consisted almost entirely of dissident queries, according to Richard Evans's recent biography.

4   An interesting twist is that his son has recently become principal of Lake View High School, my old school.

5   *Geist* should be translated more accurately as 'spirit of the times'.

6   There is a slightly earlier piece in the *University of Chicago Magazine* CVII, no. 4 (2015) by the eminent composer Philip Glass which captures beautifully the environment – this happy hunting ground for ideas and intellectual distinction.

7   Although he was not a major activist as a student, it is hard not to mention Senator Bernie Sanders, who tried to run for president in 2016 but was beaten for the Democratic nomination by Hillary Clinton and again in 2020 by Joe Biden. Bernie was in the class two years ahead of me, the son of a Polish-born paint salesman from Brooklyn. An article describes him as arriving as a transfer student in 1961 or 1962 'at a campus busy waking up from the political somnolence of the 1950s … Even in the '50s, University of Chicago was known as a hotbed of radicalism' (Rick Perlstein in the *University of Chicago Magazine* CVII, no. 3 (2015)). The Perlstein article notes very acutely Sanders's role in a sit-in in early 1962 aimed at the somewhat questionable if practical policies of the university in keeping the Hyde Park buildings it owned white. Others in my time joined the Weather Underground or other radical affinity groups. The beautiful Dohrn sisters from Milwaukee were memorable; Bernadette and her husband Bill Ayers seem to have been very friendly with Barack Obama when he first came to Chicago as a radical social worker. Plain indeed, but intelligent and forceful, was Bettina Aptheker, daughter of the ill-treated but assiduous Communist historian Herbert Aptheker.

8   Peter Lengyel, *International Social Science: The Unesco Experience* (New Brunswick and Oxford: Transaction Books, 1986). I never met him.
9   My father had kept his and occasionally wore it.
10 Wim Wertheim wrote a very attractive appreciation of Harry Benda's life in *Bijdragen tot de Taal-, Land- en Volkenkunde / Journal of the Humanities and Social Sciences in Southeast Asia* 128, nos. 2–3 (1972): 214–218.

Chapter 7 As a Student: Africa and England

1   Here I am thinking of Gwendolen Carter and her ilk. I have no doubt they were tied into the CIA but they clearly had broken with that part of the US establishment that favoured the continuation of colonial rule and apartheid in Africa. They were probably Democrats, hostile to traditional racism but eager to establish Cold War allies among the new rising class of African politicians. Their written work consisted in good part of considering the antecedents to that class in South Africa and providing a virtual who's who of their contemporary membership. Of course, the strong Communist presence at the heart of the ANC created a huge problem for them. That is why I am inclined to believe the story that it was actually the CIA that shopped Nelson Mandela in Howick and had him put away.
2   I can think of two Jewish intellectuals, one English (the late Bob Fine) and one South African (Daryl Glaser), with whom I have discussed the issue from time to time with some intensity. Jon Soske did inveigle me into writing down my views relatively recently for an American collection published by the Haymarket Press on the apartheid–Zionism comparison, which has become fashionable for activists. I mainly focused on how difficult it would be to find a solution to the Middle Eastern problem and on the contrast between the painful but so far rewarding example of bringing black and white together in one unified South Africa and the so-called two state solution in Palestine, in effect a kind of apartheid, as an answer there. I doubt that this will endear me to any activists, as this is not the easy comparison that is usually desired.

Chapter 8 The Tough Years Begin

1   Samuel Fisher Babbitt, *Limited Engagement: Kirkland College 1965–78. An Intimate History of the Rise and Fall of a Coordinate College for Women* (Indiana: XLibris, 2006), n.p. I remember him quite well but knew him only slightly in my position as a temporary assistant professor.
2   Babbitt, *Limited Engagement*, 64.
3   Babbitt, *Limited Engagement*, 282.
4   In the count of religious preference for most of the college history entrants, Babbit (p. 300) notes that 40 per cent described themselves as without any (a wildly higher figure than in the country at large), 20.9 per cent were Protestant and 19.9 per cent Jewish (this last figure also wildly higher). This probably resonated well with the teaching and administrative personnel, and, oddly enough, the students in this way were rather like many of those at the University of Chicago. They also

included girls from Hamilton-oriented families unable to access the boys' college. This generous acceptance of Jews was a hallmark of a gradual change in the early 1960s that marked the new college and was still looked at askance by the old one. See Babbit, *Limited Engagement*, 149, 161.

5   Henry was to make his career at Wesleyan University as an historian of England and is well known as a pioneer gay activist. By chance, he came from Utica, a one-time industrial city which Clinton serves as a small, distant, affluent suburb, and I got to meet his family and their friends once or twice. It is remarkable that even in a small and apparently isolated place like Utica, you could find Jews with intellectual tastes and a fairly left-wing background. Utica, unlike the bigger upstate New York cities, voted Republican; certainly the region did.

6   Tom introduced me to the fringe of the culturally avant-garde if rather dangerous world of the East Village. While I was in Nigeria, the East Village flowered as a cultural node. Keith Haring was perfecting the art of street painting at this time while Jean-Michel Basquiat, the painter, often spent the night in the drug-ridden square later in the decade. Andy Warhol was at his peak. American rock was still alive. 'Walk on the wild side …,' the Velvet Underground told us. I would walk back to Tom's flat on Avenue B very fast if I came back late at night but fortunately never experienced any difficulty. Tom took me to gay clubs, which mostly bored me, and then finally gave up on getting me excited in this way.

Chapter 9 An Intellectual and an African: Nigeria

1   The third and senior member of the team, Michael Etherton, brought up in Southern Rhodesia, wrote *The Development of African Drama* (New York: Africana Publishing Co., 1982), exposing the critical work behind the team's efforts. For some rather more original offshoots, as it were, of our expatriate existence, see the memoirs of the late radical teacher of librarianship, Ronald Benge, *Confessions of a Lapsed Librarian* (Metuchen and London: Scarecrow Press, 1984) or, on running off to the desert with the romantic Tuareg, Irish novelist Gaye Shortland, *Polygamy: A Novel* (Dublin: Poolbeg Press, 1998).

2   It would not be right to suggest that the once dominant Northern People's Congress was acceptable to all Hausa-speaking Muslims. On the contrary, in the electoral past there had been a socially radical opposition, the Northern Elements Progressive Union, which had a large support base and was aimed against the old power elite, but also with its appeal largely confined to the Northern Muslims. The British had generally done what they could to prop up the NPC, moderate from the point of view of their interests, and I remember seeing questionable things in the Archives showing what some engineered in violent ethnic confrontations. Echoes of this kind of class conflict were still to be found in my time. Perhaps later these divisions mainly shifted into struggles over the meaning of Islam. I am only aware of a few places in sub-Saharan Africa, also Muslim, where this kind of class politics also developed: Sudan and Zanzibar. In Southern Nigeria, class simply did not lead to a more social kind of political organisation.

3 The only account that does him justice for an international audience of which I am aware is a few pages in Mahmood Mamdani, *Define and Rule: The Native as Political Identity* (Cambridge: Harvard University Press, 2012).

4 In his detailed study of Nigerian historiography written in German, Wolfgang Käse describes me together with Bob and our friend, the Berkeley geographer Mike Watts, as 'red feet', who, in the course of a limited stay in Nigeria, created a proto-school that led to the emergence of a Marxist reputation for the department, which later saw a split with Islamist-oriented scholars. I wonder if we really had such an influence. Mike and Bob were PhD research students and Bob prolonged his stay by teaching for an extra couple of years. Bob moved into writing about British imperial and colonial theory once established in Canada while Mike shifted most of his focus to the Niger Delta and the oil-linked insurgencies there. I was to find that being a 'red foot' at Harvard and in my own country probably made me very unwelcome.

Chapter 10 An Intellectual and an African: Dar es Salaam and Harvard

1 There were a surprising number of pubs on this otherwise very stark campus on the outskirts of Coventry.

2 He died soon after his return to Nigeria.

3 Bill has found a home in a provincial Nigerian city where he teaches at the American University of Nigeria. I do find it interesting that he also has been happy to go out on a one-way ticket to this notoriously difficult country for foreigners.

4 A good introduction to the beginning of this student movement is Glen Moss's Johannesburg-based memoir, *The New Radicals* (Johannesburg: Jacana Media, 2014).

5 For a sympathetic view of the unions up to this point, see Steven Friedman, *Building Tomorrow Today: African Workers in Trade Unions 1970–1984* (Johannesburg: Ravan Press, 1984). The later developments are taken up by many journalists, polemical authors and academics. However, one should also note the recently published memoirs of some of the trade unionists, notably Jan Theron and John Copelyn, which capture the time and place. Quite a few of the unionists of the late 1970s and the first half of the 1980s had a stint as postgraduate students and were the authors of interesting theses. This mix of academic (very often, historian) and activist was inspiring to me.

Chapter 11 South Africa, My Home

1 An objective indicator might be the level of maths taught. In my final year of high school, I did advanced algebra and calculus. As of the 1980s, even elite schools in South Africa did not offer this. However, it should be said that this is no longer true. Of course, the standards of maths teaching in the mass of schools in predominantly black catchment areas are mostly abysmal.

2   In this period, there were in fact two law degrees possible, but the easier one to get through, which had some limitations on what you could do with it, was less desirable and, once they started to come through in small numbers, largely of interest to black students.

3   Later very prominent in Denel, the state arms manufacturer post-apartheid, and a former ambassador to Oman whom I bumped into, shortly after his sudden departure from Durban, entering the Harare post office, while I was visiting Zimbabwe.

4   For a work with an approach to which I largely adhere and with a contribution by me and some references elsewhere to my work, see Francesco Boldizzoni and Pat Hudson (eds.), *Routledge Handbook of Global Economic History* (London and New York: Routledge, 2016).

5   Professor Gourley and her chief deputy moved on to remunerative administrative jobs in England, the 'mother country' from which I imagine they are unlikely to return, when they reached this point.

Select Bibliography of Bill Freund's Publications

This bibliography is organised thematically and at the same time reflects the periodisation of Bill Freund's published works. The first two sections consist of his works on South Africa that came out of his PhD research (on the Batavian period of Cape history) and publications generated by his academic sojourns in Nigeria and Tanzania. The third section lists his South African publications and is divided thematically into the various areas and issues that he researched and wrote about. The fourth and final section, 'Reviews and overviews', includes his major books of synthesis as well as his many masterly writings that either reviewed a publication or a field or approached historiographical questions with a new eye. Each of these four sections is organised chronologically, with the earliest publications at the beginning and the most recent at the end.

1. Colonial history of South Africa

'The Cape Eastern Frontier during the Batavian Period'. *Journal of African History* XIII, no. 4 (1972): 631–645.

'The Career of Johannes Theodorus van der Kemp and His Role in the History of South Africa'. *Tijdschrift voor Geschiedenis* LXXXVI, no. 3 (1973): 376–390.

'Some Thoughts on the Study of the History of the Cape Eastern Frontier Zone'. In *Beyond the Cape Frontier*, edited by Christopher C. Saunders and Robin Derricourt, 83–99. Cape Town: Longmans, 1974.

'Race and the Social Structure of South Africa 1652–1836'. *Race and Class* XVIII, no. 1 (Summer 1976): 53–67.

'The Cape during the Transitional Era 1795–1814'. In *The Shaping of South African Society 1652–1820*, edited by Richard Elphick and Hermann Giliomee, 211–240. Cape Town: Longmans, 1979. Revised edition 1989. Translated as 'Die Kaap onder die tussentydse regerings 1795–1814'. In *'n Samelewing in wording: Suid-Afrika, 1652–1820*, edited by Hermann Giliomee and Richard Elphick. Cape Town: Maskew Miller Longman, 1982.

2. Continental African history

'Vent-for-Surplus Theory and the Economic History of West Africa'. *Savanna* (Zaria, Nigeria) VI, no. 2 (December 1977): 191–196. Written with R.W. Shenton.

'Oil Boom and Crisis in Contemporary Nigeria: Production and Exchange in a Dependent Capitalist Economy'. *Review of African Political Economy* 13 (1979): 8–20.

Review of *The Capitalist World Economy*, by I. Wallerstein. *Race and Class* XXI, no. 2 (Autumn 1979): 193–198.

'The Incorporation of Northern Nigeria into the World Capitalist Economy: A Study in the Development and Transformation of an African Social Formation'. *Review of African Political Economy* 13 (1979): 8–20. Written with Bob Shenton.

Capital and Labour in the Nigerian Tin Mines. Ibadan History Series. London: Longman, 1981.

'Class Conflict, Political Economy and the Struggle for Socialism in Tanzania'. *African Affairs* LXXX, no. 331 (October 1981): 483–499.

'Labour Migration to the Northern Nigerian Tin Mines 1903–45'. *Journal of African History* XX, no. 1 (1981): 73–84.

'Social Protest and Theft in the History of the Nigerian Tin Mines'. *Radical History Review* 26 (1982). Reproduced in *Banditry, Rebellion and Social Protest in Africa*, edited by Donald Crummey. London: James Currey, 1986.

'Nigerian Tin Mining and Imperialism: From the Niger Company to ATMN'. In *Entreprises et entrepreneurs en Afrique*, vol. I, edited by Laboratoire 'Connaissance du Tiers_Monde'. Paris: L'Harmattan, 1983.

3.1. Nation, state and politics

'South Africa: A New Nation-State in a Globalising Era?' *Transformation* 56 (2004): 41–52. Also published in *Journal of the Humanities* III (2005).

'Elite Formation and Elite Bonding: Social Structure and Development in Durban'. *Urban Forum* XV, no. 2 (2004): 134–162. Written with Shannon Moffett.

'The State of South Africa's Cities'. In *State of the Nation South Africa 2005–2006*, edited by Sakhela Buhlungu, John Daniel, Roger Southall and Jessica Lutchman, 303–332. Cape Town: HSRC Press; East Lansing, MI: Michigan State University Press, 2005.

3.2. Labour

The African Worker. Cambridge: Cambridge University Press, 1988.

'A New Industrial Revolution? Technological Change and the Implications for South African Labour'. *Social Dynamics* 18, no. 1 (1992): 1–19.

'Organized Labor in the Republic of South Africa: History and Democratic Transition'. In *Trade Unions and the Coming of Democracy in Africa*, edited by Jon Kraus, 199–228. New York and Basingstoke: Palgrave Macmillan, 2007.

'Apartheid and After: The Development of Labour Studies and Labour History in South Africa'. In *Work and Culture in a Globalized World from Africa to Latin America*, edited by Babacar Fall, Ineke Phaf-Rheinberger and Andreas Eckert, 233–252. Paris: Karthala; Berlin: Humboldt Universität, 2015.

'Work across Africa: Labour Exploitation and Mobility in Southern, Eastern and Western Africa'. *Africa* 87, no. 1 (2017): 27–35. Written with Stefano Bellucci.

'Trade Unions'. In *General Labour History of Africa: Workers, Entrepreneurs and Governments, 20th and 21st centuries*, edited by Stefano Bellucci and Andreas Eckert, 523–552. London: James Currey, 2019.

3.3. Social class and Natal's Indian population

'Indian Women in the Changing Character of the Working Class Indian Household in Natal, 1860–1990'. *Journal of Southern African Studies* 17, no. 3 (1991): 414–429.

'The Rise and Decline of an Indian Peasantry in Natal'. *Journal of Peasant Studies* XVIII, no. 2 (1991): 263–287.

Insiders and Outsiders: The Indian Working Class of Durban in the Twentieth Century. Portsmouth, NH: Heinemann; Oxford: James Currey; Pietermaritzburg: University of Natal Press, 1995.

3.4. Urban history

'The City of Durban: Towards a Structural Analysis of the Economic Growth and Character of a South African City'. In *Africa's Urban Past*, edited by David Anderson and Richard Rathbone, 144–161. Portsmouth, NH: Heinemann; London: James Currey, 2000.

'Brown and Green in Durban: The Evolution of Environmental Policy in a Post-Apartheid City'. *International Journal of Urban and Regional Research* XXV, no. 4 (2001): 717–739.

'Contrasts in Urban Segregation: A Tale of Two Cities, Durban (South Africa) and Abidjan (Côte d'Ivoire)'. *Journal of Southern African Studies* XXVII, no. 3 (2001): 527–546.

The D(urban) Vortex; A South African City in Transition. Pietermaritzburg: University of Natal Press, 2002. Co-edited with Vishnu Padayachee.

'Development in Cato Manor, Durban: Political Interpretations'. In *Urban Reconstruction in the Developing World; Learning through an International Best Practice*, edited by Jeff McCarthy and Peter Robinson, 148–152. Cape Town: Heinemann, 2004. Written with Brij Maharaj and Maurice Makhatini.

The African City: A History. Cambridge: Cambridge University Press, 2007. Chinese edition forthcoming in 2020.

'La ville sud-africaine: est-elle encore "post-apartheid"? Elements de réflexion à partir du cas de Durban'. *Revue Tiers-Monde* 196 (October–November 2008): 741–758. Published in English in revised form as 'Is There Such a Thing as a Post-Apartheid City?' *Urban Forum* XXI, no. 3 (2010): 283–298.

'Kinshasa: An Urban Elite Considers City, Nation and State'. *Journal of Contemporary African Studies* XXIX, no. 1 (2011): 33–48.

'The African City: Decolonisation and After'. In *Beyond Empire and Nation: The Decolonization of African and Asian Societies, 1930s–1970s*, edited by Els Bogaerts and Remco Raben, 241–266. Leiden: KITLV Press, 2012.

'The Modern African City and Its Antecedents'. In *The Oxford Handbook of Cities in World History*, edited by Peter Clark, 622–644. Oxford: Oxford University Press, 2013.

'African Cities: Material Life and Post-Coloniality'. *Territorio: rivista trimestrale del Dipartimento di Architettura e Studi Urbani, Politecnico di Milano* 81 (2017): 23–27. Published also in *L'Africa delle città / Urban Africa*, edited by Alessandro Gusman and Cecilia Pennacini, 3–26. Turin: Accademia Press, 2017.
'From Precolonial to Postcolonial African Cities: Identity Formation, Social Change and Conflict'. In *The City as Power: Urban Space, Place and National Identity*, edited by Alexander Diener and Joshua Hagen, 169–182. Lanham, MD: Rowman and Littlefield, 2018.

3.5. History and trajectory of development

'Development and Underdevelopment in Southern Africa: A Historical Overview'. *Geoforum* XVII, no. 2 (1986): 133–140.
'The Social Character of Secondary Industry in South Africa with Special Reference to the Witwatersrand 1915–45'. In *Organisation and Economic Change*, edited by Alan Mabin, 78–119. Johannesburg: Ravan Press, 1989.
'S.A. Gold Mining in Transformation: Change in the Social Conditions of Accumulation in the Late 1980s'. In *The South African Economic Crisis*, edited by Steve Gelb, 110–128. Cape Town: David Philip; London: Zed Press, 1991.
'South Africa: The End of Apartheid and the Emergence of the BEE Elite'. *Review of African Political Economy* 114 (2007): 661–678.
'South Africa as Developmental State?' *Africanus* (Pretoria) XXXVII, no. 2 (2007): 191–197.
'State, Capital and the Emergence of a New Power Elite in South Africa: "Black Economic Empowerment" as a Development Strategy'. In *The Aid Rush: Foreign Aid for Economic Development*, vol. II, edited by Monika Pohle and Helge Pharo, 11–49. Issues in Contemporary History series. Oslo: Oslo Academic Press, 2008.
Development Dilemmas in South Africa. Pietermaritzburg: University of KwaZulu-Natal Press, 2010. Co-edited with Harald Witt.
'The South African Developmental State and the First Attempt to Create a National Health System: Another Look at the Gluckman Commission of 1942–44'. *South African Historical Journal* LXIV, no. 2 (2012): 170–186.
'Swimming against the Tide: The Macro-Economic Research Group in the South African Transition 1991–94'. *Review of African Political Economy* 138 (2013): 519–536.
'Competition, Neo-liberalism and Twenty-First Century Capitalism: Perspective from the Cities'. In *Métropoles en débat: (dé)construction de la ville compétitive*, edited by Antoine Le Blanc, Jean-Luc Piermay, Philippe Gervais-Lambony, Matthieu Giroud, Céline Pierdet and Samuel Rufa, 395–406. Paris: Presses Universitaires de Paris Ouest, 2014.
'Post-Apartheid South Africa under ANC Rule: A Response to John S. Saul's Ideas on African Development'. *Transformation* 89 (2015): 50–75.
'The Keys to the Economic Kingdom: State Intervention and the Overcoming of Dependency in Africa: A Comparison of South Africa and Black Africa before the Crisis of the 1970s'. *Theoria* 147 (2016): 44–60.

'Industrialisation and Society: A Comparison of the Japanese Developmental State and South Africa'. *Economic Review of Kansai University* (Osaka, Japan) 67, no. 4 (2018): 1–20.

Twentieth Century South Africa: A Developmental History. Cambridge: Cambridge University Press, 2019.

4. Reviews and overviews

The Making of Contemporary Africa. Bloomington: Indiana University Press; London: Macmillan, 1984. Second edition, Boulder, CO: Lynne Rienner; London: Macmillan, 1998. Third edition 2016.

'The New South African Historiography'. *Review of African Political Economy* 29 (1984): 155–160.

The Modes of Production: A Debate in African Studies'. *Canadian Journal of African Studies* XIV, no. 1 (1985): 23–29.

'Defending South African Capitalism'. Review of *Capitalism and Apartheid*, by Merle Lipton. *Transformation* 4 (1987): 84–98.

'Western Approaches to African History' (review article). *Comparative Studies in Society and History* XXIX, no. 2 (1987): 403–407.

'Radical History Writing and the South African Context'. *South African Historical Journal* XXIV (1991): 154–159.

Review of *Commanding Heights and Community Control*, by Patrick Bond, and three other books. *South African Labour Bulletin* 16, no. 5 (May/June 1992): 78–85.

'Introduction: The Poor Whites: A Social Force and a Social Problem in South Africa'. In *White but Poor: Essays on the History of Poor Whites in Southern Africa 1880–1940*, edited by Rob Morrell, xiii–xxiii. Pretoria: Unisa Press, 1992.

'Economic History in South Africa: An Introductory Overview'. *South African Historical Journal* 34 (1996): 127–150.

'Economic History/Political Economy in South Africa: An Assessment'. In *Theory and Method in South African Human Sciences Research: Advances and Innovations*, edited by Johann Mouton, Johan Muller, Peter Franks and Themba Sono, 19–32. Pretoria: HSRC Press, 1998.

'Urban History in South Africa'. *South African Historical Journal* 52 (2005): 19–31.

'The Significance of the Mineral-Energy Complex in the Light of South African Economic Historiography'. *Transformation* 71 (2009): 3–26.

'The Union Years 1910–48'. In *The Cambridge History of South Africa*, vol. II: *1885–1994*, edited by Anne Kelk Mager, Bill Nasson and Robert Ross, 211–254. Cambridge: Cambridge University Press, 2011.

'Labour Studies and Labour History in South Africa: Perspectives from the Apartheid Era and After'. *International Review of Social History* LVIII, no. 3 (2013): 493–520.

'Reflections on the Economic History of South Africa'. In *Routledge Handbook of Global Economic History*, edited by Francesco Boldizzoni and Pat Hudson, 394–408. London: Routledge, 2015.

List of Illustrations

Unless otherwise indicated, all photographs are from the author's collection, some of which have been donated to the Leo Baeck Institute, New York.

Author's Acknowledgements

I originally thought that an autobiography was a personal project which might do me good. I then showed it to a few friends and family. I want to thank my friends David Moore, Robert Morrell, Tony Humphries and Mark Hunter for reading the first full version of this work and encouraging me to consider commercial publication. That was not the original intention. Beyond that, I have to thank the generous Wits University Press readers for their comments on which I have tried to act.

I have recently decided to give a last look at my old files with correspondence from family and friends over the years. I am really pleased to have encountered once again people who have taught me so much. I have always had a great curiosity about different milieux and different backgrounds, and my chances to get to know such a wonderful slice of human specimens, people from many countries with many different histories of their own, increased over the years. It starts with the friends from childhood and eventually reaches an astonishingly international collection. I hope I can be forgiven for not listing in the narrative so many who have been so important to me in a human sense.

Much information here comes from conversations over many decades, but let me thank two individuals who were very useful sources relatively recently. One was Jonathan Fryer, the English writer. The other was Petr Skalnik, who was kind enough to drive me around little towns in Bohemia, in Czechia, on a visit. Bill and Joe Green gave me useful corrective information on our mutual aunt Betty's family history. Much of the material used was in my personal possession. I have deposited this material at the Leo Baeck Institute in New York, thanks to the intermediation of Ray Schrag, and I make use of it with their permission. The photos had to be retrieved and given higher definition. In lockdown conditions, Dr Frank Mecklenburg, Michael Simonson and LBI German intern Melanie have done this job for me. Kira Erwin, Clive Greenstone and Rafs Mayet were lifesavers in providing technical support knowledge in Durban. For the jpeg photograph of my father's Dachau drawing, I have to thank the Dachau Memorial Archive in Germany. For the photograph of the old emperor marching in the Corpus Christi procession in front of my great-grand-father's shop, I am very grateful to Peter Prokop of the Austrian National Library. All other images belong to the Freund family archive.

Bill Freund
Durban
July 2020

Supplementary Acknowledgements

It is unusual, and sad, that a book like this comes with Supplementary Acknowledgements. These are occasioned by Bill's death in Durban in the early hours of Monday, 17 August 2020. This book is published post-humously. Virtually all of it had been written and composed before Bill died, so it remains very much a book about Bill and by Bill. But we feel that he might have liked to say a bit more if he'd known that this book was to be his swansong.

On Saturday, 22 August, Bill's family and friends from all over the world gathered virtually, by Zoom, to commemorate his life. It was an extraor-dinary affirmation of the historical and geographical length and breadth of his life and was a very moving occasion. It was attended by 173 peo-ple. It was organised and hosted by Kira Erwin, Uschi Rangan and Imraan Valodia. The following people spoke: Beth Genné, Richard Franklin, Fred Cooper, Bob Shenton, Luise White, Alan Mabin, Mike Morris, Vishnu Padayachee (who gave a reading), Shireen Hassim, Jo Beall, Rob Morrell, Jeremy Grest, Blade Nzimande and Harald Witt. David Moore opened events with a welcome, and Kira Erwin and Clive Greenstone closed pro-ceedings with an expression of thanks.

A will can tell us a lot about a person, in this case about Bill's values. In his will, Bill left bequests to the following entities: Greenpeace, Amnesty International, the KwaZulu-Natal Philharmonic Orchestra, the Durban Art Gallery, the Ubuntu Community Chest (Durban), the Association for the Aged (TAFTA), the UKZN library, and the University of KwaZulu-Natal Foundation for scholarships to students in the Social Sciences or History.

Bill would have been gratified by the recognition shown to him in the wake of his death. The following obituaries have appeared:

Keith Breckenridge, 'Bill Freund, the Academy's Outsider Insider', *New Frame*, 2 September 2020, https://www.newframe.com/bill-freund-the-academys-outsider-insider/.

Colin Bundy, 'William Mark (Bill) Freund: 1944–2020', *Africa* (forthcoming).

Shireen Hassim, 'Bill Freund: Historian, Africanist, Intellectual', *Africa Is a Country*, 4 September 2020, https://africasacountry.com/2020/09/bill-freund-historian-africanist-intellectual.

IFAS Recherche (French Institute of South Africa), http://www.ifas.org.za/research/2020/bill-freund-1944-2020/.

David Moore, 'Bill Freund 1944–2020: A Professor Who Wore the Weight of History Lightly', *The Conversation*, 14 September 2020, https://theconversation.com/bill-freund-1944-2020-a-professor-who-wore-the-weight-of-history-lightly-145652.

Robert Morrell, 'Bill Freund (1944–2020): Pioneering Economic Historian of Africa and South Africa', *Daily Maverick*, 21 August 2020, https://www.daily-maverick.co.za/article/2020-08-21-bill-freund-1944-2020-pioneering-economic-historian-of-africa-and-south-africa/.

Robert Morrell, 'Bill Freund: 6 July 1944 – 17 August 2020', *South African Journal of Science* (forthcoming).

This book was brought to completion by a fantastic team at Wits University Press, and we thank Veronica Klipp, Roshan Cader, Shaharazaad Louw, Kirsten Perkins and Corina van der Spoel, as well as Russell Martin, the copyeditor.

Robert Morrell
Cape Town
September 2020

Index

Webb, Colin 174
Webster, Eddie 162
Weil, Peter 61, 78, 82
Weintraub, Jock 77–78
Wertheim, Wim 90
Whiteread, Rachel 41
Who's Afraid of Virginia Woolf? 116
Wiener, Ronald 78
Williams, Gavin 145
Wits *see* University of the Witwatersrand
Witt, Harald *187*, 190
Wizard of Oz, The 75
Wolpe, Harold 99, 100
women
    education for 112–114, 135
    in South Africa 182
working class 57, 68, 101
Work in Progress 171
World of Yesterday, The 13
World War I 12, 14–15, 17

World War II 36–43, 56, 60, 96, 137, 144
Writing by Candlelight 144

Y
Yale University 87–93, 99, 109–111, 117
Yiddish language 97
Yudelman, David 103
Yugoslavia 25, 32

Z
Zaidi, Noorjehan 92
Zambezi River 176–177, *176*
Zaria, Nigeria 121
Zehner, Betty 23, 38
Zehner-Kerdemann family tree xii
Zimbabwe 156–157, 184
Zionism 25, 27, 37, 48, 107–108
Zolberg, Aristide 79
Zorbaugh, Harvey 58–59
Zweig, Stefan 13, 20, 52

Printed and bound by CPI Group (UK) Ltd, Croydon, CR0 4YY

09/06/2025

14685827-0001